CORNER OFFICE CHOICES

CORNER
OFFICE
CHOICES

THE EXECUTIVE WOMAN'S GUIDE TO FINANCIAL FREEDOM

BRIDGET VENUS GRIMES

LIONCREST
PUBLISHING

CORNER OFFICE CHOICES

The Executive Woman's Guide to Financial Freedom

ISBN   978-1-5445-1146-7   *Paperback*

        978-1-5445-1145-0   *Ebook*

This book is dedicated to my family—my parents, my husband, my children—for believing in me and encouraging me to pursue my passions and my dreams.

CONTENTS

INTRODUCTION...9

PART I: BEGINNING YOUR JOURNEY
1. PORTRAIT OF THE WOMAN EXECUTIVE.......29
2. THE KEY TO YOUR BEST LIFE...........................57

PART II: BUILDING YOUR BEST LIFE
3. PASSIONS AND PURSUITS...................................87
4. CASH FLOW MANAGEMENT............................103
5. BUSINESS AND CAREER MANAGEMENT......139
6. TAX STRATEGIES AND INVESTMENT
   MANAGEMENT...175

PART III: CHARTING YOUR COURSE
7. CREATE, IMPLEMENT, AND ITERATE YOUR
   ROADMAP..195
8. SUPPORT YOUR JOURNEY...............................211

CONCLUSION..231
ACKNOWLEDGMENTS...241
APPENDIX...245
ABOUT THE AUTHOR..261

INTRODUCTION

For many executive women, life is a day-to-day tightrope walk while juggling career and family. Many of these women have little time to live life on their terms, let alone have some sort of financial strategy for the future they'd like to enjoy.

After years as an executive in the financial industry, I know the biggest obstacles that stand in the way of women executives trying to live their ideal life. I also know that traditional financial planning underserves and even fails women executives. After repeatedly confronting the unique financial challenges that women executives face, I founded WealthChoice, a financial planning firm that provides advice and solutions tailored to women executives who want to craft their best life but lack the financial know-how and life planning experience to get there.

Rest assured, this is not just another dry financial how-to guide. This is a fresh approach to financial planning that encompasses not only your professional goals but also your personal goals. Far from following the traditional "one-size-fits-all" model of financial planning, this approach accommodates the specifics of your unique situation. Perhaps best of all, it allows you to live your best life today, while at the same time building a path to a secure future.

Like many women executives, you may feel as though you don't have the time or energy to master financial planning right now. Maybe it feels too overwhelming to make space in your packed schedule for one more thing. Maybe you're afraid of what you'll find if you examine your finances. Maybe you don't have hope that financial planning could have much positive impact on your daily life.

If that's how you're feeling as you pick up this book, I'd like to start by introducing you to my client Sophie. She is a woman executive living her ideal life, pursuing her personal passions while developing and thriving in her career. Not only does she enjoy her day-to-day life, but she also enjoys a deep sense of security and freedom regarding her financial reality.

But it wasn't always this way for Sophie. Before we met, she struggled with a variety of personal, professional and financial challenges. As the next section will show, Sophie was able to incrementally overcome those challenges with the help of a continuously evolving life plan.

SOPHIE'S STORY: STARTING THE JOURNEY TOWARD HOPE

I met Sophie at a business seminar that I hosted for women executives. Like most of the attendees, her life on paper looked wildly successful. Only in her mid-30s, she was an equity partner at a prestigious law firm. She was great at what she did and had a staggering income to show for it, pulling in up to $1 million annually. She was married to a man who shared her passion for travel and outdoor sports. They took great vacations every year, while splitting their time between homes in Colorado and Northern California.

However, Sophie was miserable.

Her story unfolded as we spoke after the seminar. She was working at an unsustainable pace, with no time left in her life for fun, adventure, or relaxation. Even while making money hand over fist, she felt the stress of being financially strapped. She had only $100,000 in her 401(k), not nearly enough to fund her lifestyle for a year. As we continued talking, her face, voice, and demeanor bore the evidence that she couldn't keep up this pace much longer. I'll never forget her words: "It feels like I'm on a treadmill that I can't get off."

I asked her, "How would you like your life to look, instead?"

Sophie confessed that she'd been dreaming for months about making a radical shift in her life. A few years back, she and her husband had traveled to Europe, where they'd fallen in love with a sleepy little seaside village. They imagined building a home there, right beside the water, where they wouldn't have to work as hard and could spend more time together, sharing the activities they both loved. They vowed that someday, when it made sense, they would downsize their lives and move to this village. But someday was still a long way off.

Over the next several weeks and months, Sophie and I began to meet regularly. We talked in more detail about the current state of her life. It turned out that she was working this crazy schedule because her lifestyle was considerably more expensive than it needed to be. Her home in California was a huge drain on her resources, but the demands of her client base kept her from spending more time in Colorado. Added together with the yearly vacations and the mindless spending habits she and her husband had developed, it was no wonder she felt strapped.

Our conversations had started with Sophie saying she

wanted to be able to generate the income she needed without having to work incessantly. But as we talked, her dream became more specific than that. She wanted to work a part-time schedule that would give her more flexibility with her time. She had no objection to downsizing her extravagant lifestyle, if it would allow her to spend more time doing what she loves with the person she loves.

With that in mind, we dove into the practical details around Sophie's unique vision of a perfect life. We looked at how much money she could expect to make if she scaled her work back to a part-time schedule with a handful of clients. We looked at how much she would need to have saved to retire completely by age fifty-five.

Once we knew the financial requirements around Sophie's dream life, we could put a plan together for tackling her goals one at a time. First, we designed a three-year plan for saving the cash required to build her home in Europe. Next, we determined how much she needed to live, and we used that to determine what income her part-time job would have to bring in. From there, we created a business plan for gradually winding down her practice, stepping away from her law firm and setting up her own practice, maintaining a handful of clients who would generate the income she needed to fund her downsized life. Finally, we set up a long-term plan for her to max out her 401(k) savings and save in an investment account after the house was built, so that by the time she reached age fifty-five, she'd have the option to quit work altogether.

Over the years that followed that first meeting, it was exciting to watch Sophie's strategy unfold. Today, Sophie is living in her new beachside home in the sleepy European village. She works a flexible schedule with a handful of clients who love her, while still having plenty of time to surf, go on trips, and, most importantly, relax and enjoy life with her husband. She's able to do what she's good at, while still enjoying a rich personal life.

In fact, her new flexible schedule is generating even more income than she needs to live on. But by sticking to the budget we originally designed for her, keeping cash flow under control, having a business plan that generates the income she needs, and saving for retirement so she can stop work when she'd like, Sophie is living the life she wants and is on track to keep it that way.

I see her now and then when she visits San Diego, and the difference could not be more evident. It's like a weight has been lifted off her shoulders. You can hear the confidence in her voice; her face is glowing with new peace of mind.

This is what happens when you have a financial plan.

IS CHANGE EVEN POSSIBLE FOR ME?

I constantly run into women executives who are in the same place where Sophie started. After several years climbing from one high-earning position to the next, many are still working their lives away with nothing to show for it. They spend most of the money they make, hoping it will give them the sense of satisfaction they're missing. This reckless spending pattern puts them in a place where they have to keep working at the same pace—it's the only way they can keep paying for the things they buy to reward themselves. They're caught in a cycle that makes them feel trapped in their own lives. Others are so busy that they haven't taken the time to create a plan that assures them of the financial security so that they can live the lives they want.

When I ask these women executives, "What's the purpose of all this? Why are you working so hard?" they tell me that they got into their careers for quality of life. But quality of life is exactly what they don't have.

Many of these women executives don't even know how to begin living their ideal life. They haven't spent any time looking at the ebb and flow of their finances; the job is all they know. Without a second thought, they fund all kinds of things, from new cars to a child's private school education to lavish family vacations, without knowing if they can truly afford to, and without knowing the financial implications of this spending.

When I work with these women, our conversation inevitably hinges on a single question: "What does your ideal life look like?"

Getting to that place doesn't have to happen overnight. It didn't happen that way for Sophie. We worked together for nearly ten years, discussing her goals and designing a list of action items. There were several times in those years when she would walk away with a great plan she wouldn't follow. It took her a while to get to a point where she was finally ready to do something about her situation.

For so many women executives at this high-earning level, figuring out their finances is just one more thing to do. They feel as though they have no bandwidth for learning a new skill or changing their habits, so they just shut down and do nothing.

However, for the ones who do come back, their resolve is often triggered by something very personal. They reach a point where their financial plan stops being just another task and becomes the key to the peace of mind they crave. For Sophie, we put together a plan for how she could raise the cash in three years through strategic saving, and that's when the light came on. Once she could see how to get it done, she went out and did it. As a result, her life today looks radically different. It should look different—it's *her* life. A slowed-down existence in a little corner of the world isn't everybody's ideal life, but for Sophie, it's everything she wants.

FAILURES OF THE TRADITIONAL FINANCIAL INDUSTRY

Traditional financial planning has not focused on the unique challenges faced by women executives. By not planning for these challenges, it absolutely affects these women's ability to live life on their terms.

My prior firm focused primarily on retirement planning, typical among wealth management firms. But that does not allow for planning for the many competing goals women in the thick of life have. We want to plan to live a good life now, and in the future.

Traditionally, financial planning is a very male-dominated industry. Of the 80,000 CERTIFIED FINANCIAL PLANNER™ professionals, 77 percent are male, while 23 percent are female.[1] Perhaps as a result of this, it's not uncommon for an advisor to speak mainly to the male spouse when creating a financial plan for a couple, even when the woman brings in 50 percent or more of the couple's income.

---

[1]   CFP Board, "CFP Professional Demographics, CFP Certificant Profile." (February 28, 2018) https://www.cfp.net/news-events/research-facts-figures/cfp-professional-demographics

Women executives face unique challenges in life, as well as in business, and these unique challenges must be taken into account for financial planning if these women are to have effective solutions that serve them in reaching their goals.

These unique challenges come down to four major derailers of financial success:

1. Lack of Goal Clarity
2. Failure to Manage Cash Flow
3. Failure to Strategically Manage Business and Career
4. Lack of a Comprehensive, Goal-Oriented Life Plan

Of the derailers listed above, you may find that only one or two of them apply to your life right now. Maybe you're great at cash flow management, but you don't have a plan for leveraging your career. No matter what your current financial situation looks like, this book will give specific tools and step-by-step guidance in setting up a plan that gets you wherever you want to go.

Just as every woman executive's ideal life looks different, every woman executive has different factors that trigger her to start the work needed to make that life a reality. Sometimes that trigger comes in the form you'd least expect. In my case, it came from a combination of divorce, debt, and a house that burned to the ground.

MY STORY

I started in the financial industry right out of college, working for a hedge fund in Manhattan. After several years, I decided to try something new and left my New York City financial career for work as a chef in Paris, France; New York City; and the Bay Area of California.

Marriage and kids provided a good opportunity to take some time away from work. But after three years, I was ready to enter the workforce again and took a job in corporate sales.

Eventually, though, life proved to be less than what it seemed, starting with our marriage. When it became clear that our relationship problems weren't going to work out, I began to look into how we could split our one life into two. I had a decent job, and I didn't want any money from him. I just wanted us to part ways amicably so that we could co-parent in the healthiest way possible.

But when I looked into our finances, I discovered that much of our lifestyle was being financed through debt. I was surprised, to say the least. I had spent years in the financial industry, yet I had made the choice along the way to not be engaged in my own finances.

Not long after that, a wildfire swept through our community in Southern California, destroying our home along with countless others. Because I had chosen ignorance instead of active participation in my family's finances, I was left to figure out how to rebuild life from the ground up, while continuing to work and parent.

The one thing that helped was knowing that I wasn't alone. Two of my girlfriends were going through almost the same struggles as me. In the midst of those struggles, none of us had time to look past the present moment; we were just trying to make it from one day to the next. For the first time, I realized how many smart, accomplished women must be in similar straits as me. They might not be dealing with fires or divorce, but they were overloaded with responsibilities—barely balancing the demands of their professional lives with their personal lives—and didn't have the time to figure out a plan for their finances.

I thought, "There has to be someone who can take care of these women who are so busy taking care of everyone else." That was the catalyst I needed to leave my corporate sales job and reenter the world of financial planning.

WHO IS THIS BOOK FOR?

Maybe, like Sophie, you've awakened to the reality that the life you're living now isn't the great life you envisioned when you started your career. Maybe everything seems fine right now, but you crave the peace of mind that comes from knowing that you are financially okay. Maybe you want to make sure the great life you have created stays great, but you don't know how to do that. If so, this book is written just for you.

On the other hand, you may have read this far and become aware that you don't have a plan at all. Don't let this make you feel ashamed, discouraged, or defeated. This book is not meant to point out all the ways you've failed. It's meant to give you hope by showing that any woman executive, no matter how her finances might look today, can use her money to build a path that takes her anywhere she might want to go. Your ideal life really is within your reach. All you need is a plan to achieve it.

A NOTE TO FELLOW FINANCIAL PLANNERS

As planners, we have an opportunity to support each other in helping our clients live a better life. This approach has made a difference to the women I've advised, and I hope that it will help other planners serving the same women executives.

I've designed this book to help you understand the steps involved in creating a successful financial plan, and why each step is important. But I understand that it can be daunting to implement all these steps on your own. At any point while you read, don't hesitate to reach out to a financial planner who can help you create a plan based off the content of this book.

You should also know that you're not alone on this journey, even though many women executives suffer from financial anxiety and tend to feel tremendous shame about it, believing they're the only ones who struggle in this way. They think they should have known better, that they should be in a different place, that everyone else is happier and more secure than they are.

However you feel about your life and finances today— anxious, embarrassed, uncertain, terrified, defeated, or simply dissatisfied—you need to know that thousands of smart, hardworking women share those feelings alongside you. This book is meant to give you more than just practical steps to get your finances on a good footing. It's also meant to help you live your ideal life, life on your terms, with the peace of mind that comes from financial security and being on track. That's why I've included numerous stories in this book about women executives just like you, who came to me in every kind of financial situation you can imagine. No matter what shape they were in, if the woman was ready to put the work into creating and following a plan, she was able to get on her feet and dramatically improve her quality of life.

I find that often women executives don't realize the power

of small, incremental change. Instead, many women view financial planning the way they view fitness or weight loss: it's an all-or-nothing proposition. If their effort doesn't "fix" the problem in a few days, they feel as though it's not working at all. If they stray from the plan for a day or two, they feel as though they've washed out all the progress they made.

For women who have accomplished so much in their careers, it can be hard to give themselves permission to make incremental progress toward their financial goals. That's why it's so important to celebrate the little victories along the way. Individually, those victories might not represent thousands of dollars, but what they do represent is choice. By spending a few hundred dollars less on entertainment or a car payment, and instead putting that money into your retirement account, what you've done is take charge of your money. You've made the decision to prioritize what's really important to you.

Those small decisions pave the way from where you are to where you want to be. The path to financial success is long and winding; it's in looking back after six months or a year that you see how far you've come.

After helping hundreds of women executives manage millions of dollars, I've realized that real wealth comes down to living life on your own terms. There's no specific number attached to happiness or quality of life; it's all about the choices we make. That's the reason I named my firm WealthChoice. Everything you do is a choice—the way you spend your money, the direction you take your career, the order in which you take each action in your day. (And how lucky are we to have this much choice in living our lives?) Realizing the power of choice makes all the difference for women. It breaks them free from that trapped feeling.

Moreover, choice imbues spending with personal significance. When I create a budget for a client, I'm not telling them how to spend their money. I'm simply making them aware of where it's been going, where the pitfalls are for them, and where their money should be redirected if they want their life to include the things they've said are important to them. They can implement the budget, follow some of it, throw the whole thing in a drawer and ignore it—it's up to them. It's the choice that makes all the difference. Their money is no longer a mysterious force with a mind of its own. They're the ones telling it what to do.

Quality of life comes down to getting off that treadmill and reclaiming the power of choice over your money. As a woman executive, you have the power to make your life look exactly how you want it to look. To get started, all you have to do is stop for a moment and ask yourself, "Okay, what do I want?"

PART I

BEGINNING YOUR JOURNEY

A FRESH TAKE ON FINANCIAL SECURITY AND LIVING LIFE ON YOUR TERMS

CHAPTER ONE

PORTRAIT OF THE WOMAN EXECUTIVE

Women executives confront unique issues around money that impact how their financial security may evolve. These women are intelligent, driven, high achievers and high earners. Many of them function as the family breadwinner. They are both incredibly accomplished and incredibly busy. They are also frequently anxious, tired, and overwhelmed. They have too much on their plates, not enough time to deal with it all, and are embarrassed to ask for help. Despite how hard they work, many are not living their best lives right now. And they do not realize they are not the only ones in this place.

These stories may help you recognize your own financial challenges, as well. They highlight the four biggest "derailers" of women's financial security.

EVELYN'S STORY: THE REAL COST OF YOUR GOALS

Evelyn works constantly, running a company of about ten employees, while her husband is a stay-at-home dad. She makes good money, but the two of them spend it like water. She feels that her hard work should entitle her family to a certain lifestyle, refusing to recognize that it's a lifestyle they simply can't afford. On top of paying for a brand new house and a new Mercedes, they're also dealing with $200,000 of student loan debt that they've barely put a dent in.

When Evelyn and her husband sat down with me, I asked them what they want their life to look like. They had a list of things they wanted to fund: private school and college for their child, a month off each year to travel, expansion of her company. I had to explain to them that with their current lack of cash flow management, none of these things were within their reach. Not only were their current expenses underwritten by debt, but Evelyn was even denied a business loan by her banker because her credit was so bad. The evidence was right in front of them, but they just couldn't see it.

JANINE'S STORY: THE REAL COST OF YOUR JOB

Janine is fifty years old, single, never married, with no kids. She's a partner at a law firm where she makes about $1 million per year. Throughout her life, she's managed to save money very well, and she's on track to retire in five more years.

Right now, though, she works incredibly hard, sometimes to her own disadvantage. As a woman partner in a male-dominated firm, she feels that she has to. Because she's a single woman with no family, her partners tend to assume that she has unlimited availability for whatever the firm might require. When they needed somebody to move to another city for two years—with no extra compensation or benefits—they looked to Janine. And she said yes, as she always does.

The reason for this is that Janine is terrified of losing her job. More specifically, she is terrified of losing her income. Even though she wants to retire badly, it's nerve-racking for her to picture pulling the trigger and walking away from her steady paycheck. Despite how much she works and how well she saves, she has never managed her career in a way that assures her of being financially okay once she chooses to quit working.

This financial anxiety deeply impacts her quality of life. Every year when her review comes up, she's convinced that her firm is going to cut her loose. No matter how many times she says yes when she really wants to say no, she is never fully confident of her value. Her uncertainty about finances piles up on top of the stress in her job, driving her to constantly overperform.

MELISSA'S STORY: THE IMPORTANCE OF HAVING A PLAN

Melissa is a young executive at a tech firm. Though she's just a few years into her career, she's already making great money. She's unmarried, but shares a home and lifestyle with her partner. Everything in her life is great—health, income, living situation, future prospects. But Melissa found herself wondering if she was on track to keep living this life that she loves so much.

What Melissa really wanted was assurance that her hard work today was paying forward into her future. The peace of mind she craves doesn't come from making more money or even saving more money. It comes from having a clear set of goals and a strategic plan for achieving them.

THE EMOTIONAL REALITY OF LIFE WITHOUT A PLAN

All of these people are super successful, at least on paper. They have made it to the top level of their professions, or are on their way there, some of them at the cost of their personal lives. They got where they are through intelligence, strategic decision-making, and knowing how to perform well under pressure. But all that pressure leaves them with no time or energy to enjoy their lives or plan for their future. No wonder they feel as though they're on a treadmill.

Despite the difference in circumstances amongst Evelyn, Janine, and Melissa, they all share the same deep desire to be financially secure and live life on their terms. They want to know for sure that their hard work and sacrifices are bringing them the life they want, or at least getting them closer to it. Right now, though, they're not living life on their terms.

What they don't realize is that their situation, and the emotional distress they experience around it, could change dramatically for the better in just a matter of months. If these folks began to manage their cash flow, leveraged their careers strategically, and made intentional choices with their financial resources, they'd have the peace of mind they long for. They would feel empowered and in control of their lives. But learning how to do that feels overwhelming to them. It's just one more item in a schedule that's already overloaded, so they don't make time for it. They stay on the same old treadmill, hoping that somehow things will eventually be different for them.

This is the case for a lot of women out there. They work incredibly hard and feel that should justify them getting what they want, when they want it. But because they never take the time to articulate their goals or create a plan around how to achieve them, these women end up trapped in a cycle of earning and spending. As a result, they can never scale back their hours or retire when they intended to. They have nothing to show for a lifetime of effort.

Women in this situation feel very isolated. Sharing the truth about their financial situation, even with their closest friends or family, makes them feel too vulnerable. Because money is such a powerful measure of our self-worth, there's a lot of shame associated with acknowledging that our finances aren't in a good place.

KEEPING UP WITH THE JONESES

A paper published in the journal *Motivation and Emotion* by Knox College psychology professor Tim Kasser determined that when people become more materialistic, their emotional well-being suffers. Instead of making us happier, spending more money has the opposite effect: "When we're feeling insecure, we orient towards materialistic solutions. We live in a culture that continually tells us our worth is based on our bank account. Our consumer-driven society equates financial success with keeping up with the Joneses. But the connection between our stuff and our self-esteem is a two-way street. If we become less materialistic, our well-being will improve. If our well-being improves, we become less materialistic."[2]

Living under the pretense of wealth breeds a quiet form of desperation that can bring people to the breaking point. No house, no car, and no bonus check can compare to the genuine peace of mind that comes when you *know* you can fund the things that are genuinely important to you.

---

2   Kasser,T., Rosenblum, K.L., Sameroff, A.J. et al. "Changes in materialism, change in psychological well-being: Evidence from three longitudinal studies and an intervention experiment." Motiv Emot (2014) 38:1. https://doi.org/10.1007/s11031-013-9371-4

WOMEN'S UNIQUE CONSIDERATIONS AROUND MONEY

No matter what industry you work in, being a woman in that industry will bring unique challenges that men don't have to deal with. The response isn't to resign ourselves, nor is it to get overly caught up in fighting for systemic change. Instead, the most constructive approach is to identify what those challenges are and get the resources you need to overcome them.

COMPETING GOALS

Women executives tend to take on responsibilities without considering their long-term costs. For most of us, this is just second nature—women are incredibly giving, even to their own detriment. As a result, they end up with a whole host of competing financial goals. At the same time that they are working toward retiring at a reasonable age, they also want to take care of their aging parents, while at the same time helping to support their grown children and grandchildren.

One couple I know had chosen to downsize their lifestyle shortly after their kids left for college. But only a few years after selling their home and buying a smaller one, I learned that they were once again in the market, this time for a bigger house. The reason? Their two children, now adults, were moving back in with them. Both these children work and make good money; nevertheless, this couple is not only housing them rent-free, but they cover a great deal of their expenses. They feel obligated to continue helping their children, but they're doing it at the cost of their own financial security.

Women executives seldom realize how this pattern of saying yes to various obligations contributes to their stress, anxiety, and feeling trapped. They put their personal goals on the back burner, funding everything except the things that contribute to their own happiness. We see time and time again that women choose to put others before themselves—to their financial detriment.

My job is to help these women executives understand that their current way of life is a choice and to help them see what other choices are available to them. What do they need for their own life? What does quality of life mean to them, and what's involved in creating it? It's important for women executives to recognize that no matter where they start, there's only so much time they have left, and only so much money they can make within that time frame. It's vital to understand the long-term implications of how they choose to use their resources.

LESS MONEY TO FUND THEIR GOALS

We're all familiar with the fact that women executives are

paid less than men for doing the same jobs. A lesser known fact is that the average woman executive leaves a million dollars on the table over the course of her working life, simply by not knowing how much she is worth or asking for what she deserves.[3] How is this possible?

By Getting Paid Less

By not getting paid what you're worth, you don't get the opportunity to save as much as you should. That translates to lost income, lost social security benefits (which are scaled on your pay), and lost portfolio growth over time.

By Not Negotiating

Where men generally have no problem asking (or over-asking) for what they are worth, women seem instinctively averse to it. Moreover, women executives often don't know the market value of their work—women report salary expectations between 3 percent and 32 percent lower than those of men for the same jobs.

Failing to negotiate plays a significant role in wage disparity. A study from Carnegie Mellon University revealed that eight times as many men as women graduating with a master's degree negotiated the starting salary of their first

---

3   Linda Babcock and Sara Laschever, *Women Don't Ask: Negotiation and the Gender Divide.* (Princeton University Press, 2003.)

job. That first job sets the tone for your earning potential over your entire career—by not negotiating, a woman stands to lose over $500,000 by age sixty.

By Not Obtaining Sponsors

In addition, women executives are less likely to get the benefit of powerful sponsors that can help them climb to higher-paid positions in their field. All this means less money to fund their goals.

By Working Less

Not only do women executives make less money than men in the same position, but they work fewer hours over the course of their career. On average, a woman executive's working life is twelve years shorter than a man's, mainly because they take time off where men typically don't—for pregnancy and recovery, for raising children, for tending to older parents. Women executives also tend to retire sooner, either because they're exhausted or because their health won't allow them to continue at the same pace. Again, this twelve-year gap translates into a tremendous loss of income.

By Taking Time Off

Some of my clients, after taking time off for pregnancy,

will go back to work at a reduced schedule or workload in order to have time for raising their children. However, they soon find that because they've cut down their schedule by 10 to 20 percent, the company is sticking them with the projects that nobody else wants. This downgrade doesn't just affect their income; it also affects their career trajectory. Having low-profile projects means less ability to position yourself for promotions and raises.

By Putting Themselves Last

It can't be denied that women executives have a significant tendency to make sacrifices that prioritize their personal life over the professional. Regardless, we make these choices without thinking twice, and we take the consequences in relative silence.

As for fighting the system to get the financial rewards we deserve, it feels like just one more thing to do.

MORE PROFESSIONAL CHALLENGES

The nature of women's professional challenges varies, depending on the industry. But those challenges all come down to the rewards and motivations that brought them into those careers.

From focus groups I have conducted, I've learned that

many women attorneys tend to pursue law because they expect it will offer them a high standard of living, while women executives in science, technology, engineering, and mathematics (STEM) are drawn to these fields out of passion for those particular studies. Women attorneys are beset by the challenge of earning the same pay as their male counterparts. Women in STEM have to work extra hard to attain positions that routinely go to men. Statistically, women in STEM get passed over for leadership roles and are funneled into administrative positions instead. Even there, women come up against a glass ceiling. Women make up only 15 percent of the chief officer titles in the technology industry, and more than 30 percent of public companies and 68 percent of unicorn tech companies have no women on their boards.[4] Women executives are not making it to senior positions because they lack the sponsors to help them get there. In their report Sponsoring Women to Success, Catalyst found that sponsorships are key to advancing high performers and give them greater opportunities to excel through skill development and increased visibility. It is believed that having a sponsor rather than a mentor explains the gaps in career advancement and compensation that women face right out of the gate, as well as over time, in comparison to their male peers.

Another example of the unique challenges professional

---

4   "Breaking down the gender challenge," McKinsey Quarterly, (March 2016)

women face can be found in medicine. Although women outnumber men among degree earners in the life sciences, and women comprise 37 percent of all physicians and surgeons, only 16 percent are permanent medical school deans.[5] Even in the more traditional female role of nursing, while women continue to make up the majority of registered nurses (89.4 percent) and nurse practitioners (90 percent), a recent study showed that male nurses were earning more than women![6] There exists a clear gender pay gap here, even in traditionally female roles.[7]

This didn't happen just because the medical industry favors men. According to a recent study, male nurses were awarded higher salaries *because they asked for them*. For whatever reason, one of the greatest professional challenges women face is their own tendency to tell themselves they aren't ready for the next move, that they haven't proven themselves sufficiently, or that they haven't earned the right to ask for more.

POST-CAREER EXPENSES

So in addition to the fact that women take time off work for caregiving, spend fewer years working, wind up with

---

5   "The Women's Leadership Gap," Center for American Progress (May 21, 2017).

6   US Bureau of Labor Statistics Table 11 Current Population Survey: Household data annual average 2015.

7   "Even in Nursing Women are Paid Less than Men," Huffington Post, accessed May 24, 2015.

less social security, and earn less relative to men, key life expenses like retirement and healthcare are more expensive for them.

We have longevity to partially thank for that. The average woman lives two years longer than a man does, which means she has more years of life to fund. Women also tend to serve as the caregivers to their spouses in old age, a role that has considerable financial and emotional costs. From reduced working hours for caregiving, which translates into lost wages and social security benefits (to the tune of $324,044), to the physical and emotional tolls it creates, caregiving can have a tremendous cost for women.[8]

Outliving your spouse has additional financial challenges for women. Social security benefits may be reduced, and pensions and annuity income may be affected, depending on the chosen income distribution. Unfortunately, many life costs do not decrease enough to offset the decrease in income. Add to this the change in tax filing status to "single," and you are looking at some significant income challenges.

That's not all. Women's healthcare costs are statistically more expensive than men's. In fact, due to longevity, a healthy fifty-five-year-old woman on average will pay $79,000 more for healthcare over her retirement than

8   "Women and Caregiving: Facts and Figures," Family Caregiver Alliance.

a fifty-five-year-old man.[9] Once they are alone in old age, they must figure out how to pay these costs with limited funds, as well as create a plan for getting the long-term care they need, since they don't have the benefit of a spouse to serve as their caregiver. There is a host of financial issues around getting older as a single woman, and many women don't take the time to plan or save for these issues.

It's no wonder that only 10 percent of women are "very confident" in their ability to fully retire with a comfortable lifestyle.[10] Just like Janine, they keep putting off their last day on the job, because they don't know how much they're going to need when that day comes. For many of them, there's good reason for that fear: women executives are shown to save less money over their lifetime. This inability to save is rooted in a lack of financial literacy—women in general just don't know enough about money. Often, it is because they weren't raised to understand money very well. Everything they do know is self-taught. Factor in that confidence gap that makes women executives constantly doubt their own qualifications, and you end up with a personal finance situation that is ripe for being derailed.

9   "Women's HealthCare Table in Retirement: $79,000 more than Men's," Money, December 7, 2016.

10   "Seventeen Facts About Women's Retirement Outlook," Catherine Collinson (March 2017).

FOUR DERAILERS TO WOMEN'S FINANCIAL SUCCESS

As mentioned earlier, there are four major derailers that affect the financial success of women professionals. Let's dig deeper into each of those derailers and talk about the ways that financial planning can get women executives like you on the path to living your ideal life.

DERAILER #1: LACK OF GOAL CLARITY

Oftentimes, the decisions we make around money are the decisions we *don't* make. For most of my clients, being a full-time professional as well as a spouse and parent leaves them with no time to think through what they want their life to look like down the road. As for my younger clients, they just don't see the importance of thinking that far into the future, until the future suddenly catches up with them.

I recently began working with Cara, a woman in her early thirties who works in a high-earning position at a tech company in Silicon Valley. She lives with a partner who also works, and together they make a lot more money than they need to live on. To their credit, they are both pretty frugal, live a modest lifestyle, and don't overspend. Last year, though, Cara's father died. Like many women, her mother didn't have a plan in place for taking care of herself alone.

Cara came to me and said that she'd like to have her

mother move in with her. It's a good thought, but it's not clear whether Cara can afford to fund this goal. Before this, her finances were all on autopilot. Now, she has to think about buying a house with room for her mom to share in a way that makes them both comfortable. She has to find out how much long-term care costs in California, and how long she has to project those expenses—will her mother live another ten years, or will it be more like twenty? She has to consider how this change will affect not only the happy life she enjoys now but her ideas about how she wants the next ten years to look.

I often look back and ask myself why, after being in finance for years, I didn't take a hand in managing my own family's money. The answer is because I didn't want to; it was one more thing to do, and I wanted to believe that my ex-husband had it all under control. It wasn't until life made me deal with it that I finally stepped up to the plate.

In the same way, women executives feel as though they don't have the time or the bandwidth to think through their finances, so they make the choice to keep saying "not right now." It's a choice that comes back to hurt us in the end.

That's why I start every client meeting by asking this question, "In a perfect world, how would you like your life right now to look—personally, professionally, and financially?"

If you're like a lot of women executives, you may have a hard time answering this question. You are way too busy trying to keep up with the demands of today; imagining a perfect life is a luxury you just don't have.

However, without knowing what's really important to you, you cannot have a plan of action for getting there. That's why I make my clients think through the smallest details that would help them feel happy, confident, secure, and fulfilled. If they say, "I don't want to work so much," we talk in detail about how much they do want to work. If they say, "I want to stop renting and buy a home," I ask them to describe what kind of home they want, where they want it to be, and how big a down payment they want to make.

There's a reason for this level of detail. When women executives take the time to figure out what is really important to them, they can determine what is possible now and in the future, to prioritize the goals, and then to put a plan in place for achieving their ideal life.

DERAILER #2: FAILURE TO MANAGE CASH FLOW

The women executives I work with are all high-earners, not to mention extremely intelligent and strategic when it comes to performing their jobs. However, time constraints and lack of engagement often mean that they have little awareness of where their money is going.

There is no reason why they can't live within their means. Nevertheless, a big part of my role is helping these women executives identify where they spend their money.

When I sit down with a client, after we've gone through their goals for their life, I give them a spreadsheet with three categories: income, fixed expenses, and discretionary spending. I ask them to write down where they spend their money each month. Interestingly enough, after they've estimated their spending in each category, many clients wind up with a surplus of money left over. There's a disconnect between what they think they're spending and what's actually leaving their checking account each month.

"Managing cash flow" is just industry speak for repairing this disconnect. It means making women executives aware of where their money goes each month. We have a whole process around mastering cash flow in incremental steps. First, we simply observe the money coming and going, usually for a month or two. Once we see the patterns, we begin implementing small but significant changes that redirect that cash flow toward the client's goals. Over time, these small changes yield huge savings that allow the client to fund things that are important to them. The bottom line in cash flow management is empowerment through choice—when you choose to be aware of where you're currently spending money, you can choose to spend it in a way that supports the life you want to live.

Years ago, I met a woman who, together with her husband, saved every dime they earned for their eventual retirement. Their goal was to travel the world together, and they denied themselves a lot of short-term pleasures with that in mind. Sadly, just weeks after her husband retired, he passed away. Tears ran down her face as she shared with me how she was forcing herself to take the trips they had planned. I could feel her regret at traveling alone to the places they were supposed to visit together, while trying not to reflect too much on how they'd put off really living until it was too late.

I don't believe we should put off every present source of joy for the sake of our future plans. But there needs to be a balance between enjoying life today and strategizing on how we can continue enjoying life down the road.

DERAILER #3: FAILURE TO MANAGE YOUR CAREER ACTIVELY AND STRATEGICALLY

As a woman executive, the compensation and the quality of life provided by your career or business funds your personal, professional, and financial goals. You are in the unique position of having the opportunity to have your career work for you the way you want, so that you can live the life you want.

Leveraging your career means more than simply angling for a raise or a promotion. It means using your current position to achieve the quality of life you desire. It means knowing how much you're worth and negotiating to secure that salary. It means having a plan in place about where you want your career to take you, whether it's retiring early, running your department, or pivoting to a completely different career. For business owners, it means knowing how best to leverage your business for this same quality of life and compensation.

There's no denying that as a woman, you face unique barriers and challenges to achieving the level of success you want. However, I encourage my women executive clients toward a purely practical, proactive outlook. You can't always make the playing field change for you, but you can change the way you play on it.

Derailer #3 is about acknowledging what your challenges are and finding solutions to achieve whatever success means to you. Whatever you might want—a raise, a promotion, a better schedule—you can create a plan for addressing the obstacles that stand between you and those objectives.

DERAILER #4: NOT HAVING A PLAN OF ACTION

This final derailer wraps the first three together. A lot of women executives spend their early years strategizing about how to get to the highest level they can achieve in their industry. They do this believing that getting to that level will bring them the accolades, the vocational fulfillment, and, of course, the financial rewards that will let them live life on their terms.

Once they arrive at that upper level, though, the reality is sometimes less fulfilling than they expected. Alternatively, they may work in that career for ten or twenty years, only to wake up one day and find that it's no longer satisfying to them.

In either case, these women executives don't have the bandwidth to figure out a plan for transitioning. They've put everything they have into getting to where they are; all they can think to do is stay on the track they're on.

What I want to tell these women executives is that change is so much easier than they realize. When I hear them express their feeling of being trapped, I say, "Let's step back and talk about what's really important to you. What would you like your life to look like?"

For a lot of women executives, imagining their best life is incredibly difficult to do. They've been making do and keeping up for so long that the idea of pinpointing what's really important to them feels next to impossible. Even if they could find the time to sit down and come up with a plan, it feels completely overwhelming to figure out one more thing.

It can't be denied that planning takes effort. But once you get started on the process, the effects are truly amazing.

DIANE'S STORY: ENGAGEMENT IS ESSENTIAL TO SUCCESS

I work with a woman named Diane who is in her 60s, older than the majority of my clients. Despite the success of her company, she suffered from some serious financial setbacks in the past. From our first meeting, I could tell she was going to be a tough case. Her struggles had made her cynical, unwilling to engage with the process, and skeptical that anything could significantly help her at this point. Frankly, even I was a little skeptical—I remember wondering, *Am I going to be able to help this woman?*

I am so excited about where Diane is today. She works closely with a business coach, who helps her run her firm efficiently and profitably. We were able to retrain her habits around spending and even got her to commit to a budget that we've continued to refine. We put together a team of trusted advisors to help implement the plan we created for her.

We created a variety of different retirement options for

her; at this point, she's saved hundreds of thousands of dollars, which will allow her to stop work at age seventy-five. While that's a long time to keep working, it's a doable plan that gets her where she wants to go. In the next eight years, she'll have paid off the mortgage on her house, which will allow her to scale back her workload over the succeeding five years.

By knowing that she is on track to retire when she'd like and that she has a business plan that is working for her, Diane now enjoys a more livable work schedule that gives her time to pursue her passions. She's an avid gardener and cyclist, and now that she gets to work a little less, she can live her best life today while staying on track for future financial milestones. She feels so good about where she is now, compared to where she was just two years ago. She is proof that no matter where you are in terms of living your ideal life, spending time to put a plan together can have terrific results.

Like everyone I work with, Diane's success didn't happen overnight. She had to commit to the process, which meant allowing herself to be vulnerable with me. In our meetings, she revealed everything about her background that contributed to her situation—a bankruptcy, a divorce, bad spending habits, all the sources of embarrassment or guilt that keep people in a financial straitjacket. By bringing those things to light, she's become empowered to make the choices that lead her to a different place, and that has brought her so much confidence. She's seen that she does have the capacity to build the life she wants.

As a result, she's become one of my biggest supporters, constantly connecting me with other people she thinks could benefit from financial planning. I always remind her that I'm not the one who worked the magic in her life. She did it herself, through her willingness to articulate the life that would make her happy, create a plan for how to get there, and follow those steps one day at a time.

Once you've identified where you would like to be, you work on building a path to get there from where you are now. What are the gaps in the road between your present reality and the best life you can envision? What are the solutions available for filling in those gaps?

Next, you write this plan of action down. There are some impressive statistics showing that if you have a plan on paper, your chances of success are much greater. A study by Dominican University of California[11] revealed that for people who actually wrote down their goals, their success over ten years was exponentially greater than

---

11   "Study Backs up Strategies for Achieving Goals," Dominican University of California, http://www.goalband.co.uk/uploads/1/0/6/5/10653372/strategies_for_achieving_goals_gail_matthews_dominican_university_of_california.pdf.

those of folks who thought about their goals but never wrote them down.

The most important piece of the life plan is, of course, action. You don't conquer your life plan all at once. Instead, you have a sequence of incremental actions that you tackle one by one.

Life plans, like life itself, constantly evolve. You don't just have this plan and set off into the sunset toward your perfect world. Things happen all the time that require your life plan to readjust.

For example, a client just called me yesterday to let me know the latest change in her life plan: she's getting married. Our whole plan was designed around her income as a single woman, but now she is planning to share income, expenses, and hopefully down the road, children with her new husband. That changes a lot of things about the order of her priorities and the time horizons for getting them done. However, having her life plan on paper makes it much easier to reconfigure around these new elements. She's able to see how to adjust her lifestyle to keep moving toward her goals, as opposed to starting all over.

THE BOTTOM LINE

For women executives, living your ideal life is absolutely

possible if you have a plan for the four biggest derailers. At the end of the day, it comes down to simple awareness and having a plan for living life on your terms. Where are you right now? What are the obstacles between you and your ideal life? What are you going to do about them? Even if that awareness leaves you feeling anxious or ashamed, I can promise you that you're not alone. There's nothing you're dealing with that can't be solved by making small, incremental changes. By being aware, you have the ability to choose how successful you want to be. That's what it means to live your life on your own terms.

CHAPTER TWO

THE KEY TO YOUR BEST LIFE

In this chapter, you'll learn the key features of the novel approach I have developed to address the primary financial derailers for women executives like you. This approach encompasses not just the financial component of your life but all aspects of life, including your personal and professional goals and pursuits. This approach is highly successful for the very reasons it differs from the traditional financial planning approach: in addressing the major financial derailers women executives face, it recognizes the challenges specific to women. Best of all, this approach is incremental, choice-driven, collaborative, and individually tailored (rather than being one-size-fits-all).

As we get started, I want to encourage you, as I encourage all my clients, to embark on your journey to financial well-being with courage. When you choose to engage wholeheartedly with this new approach to financial planning, you will immediately experience, maybe for the first time in a long time, real hope that the life you want is within your reach. While the process is incremental, the benefits are immediate. To illustrate that truth, let me share stories from two of my clients who experienced that "aha!" moment when they engaged with this new financial planning approach.

BRENDA'S STORY: CHOOSING YOUR OWN PATH

As a chief of staff at a major international corporation, Brenda made a good income but didn't feel fully satisfied. She dreamed of a more relational job, one that would let her invest in people on a face-to-face level. She also wanted a less demanding workload that would allow her to make her own schedule, work at a gentler pace, and maybe even take a few days off to spend with her kids.

By the time Brenda met with me, she had narrowed her dreams down to two very different possibilities. The first was starting a new career as a business coach for executives like herself. The second was exiting the corporate world altogether and opening a little neighborhood flower shop, not so much for the income but to satisfy a passion of hers.

Brenda's goals weren't terribly lofty, but they were none-theless challenging. To start with, Brenda was a single mom with two kids to support. Quitting her current job to start a brand new enterprise simply wasn't an option for her.

While Brenda's management expertise made coaching a natural choice of vocation, it didn't promise a smooth transition. She had no background or credentials in coaching, no client base to whom she could begin marketing herself, and no experience in building a business from the ground up.

The flower shop idea had all the same obstacles as business coaching, with the added challenges unique to the retail industry. It was clear that no matter which direction she chose, it would probably leave her without an adequate income for quite some time.

To top it all off, Brenda's dreams were also burdened by a significant amount of debt. Lack of planning and mindless spending had put her current finances in the red. Despite her significant salary, she routinely found herself looking forward to her annual bonus as a way to pay bills and level out the debt she had accumulated throughout the year. It was obvious that cash flow management was a challenge for her.

Fortunately, when Brenda came to me for planning, she

brought a practical mindset along with her big dreams. She accepted the place she was starting from and understood that in order to create the life she wanted, she had to be ready to make changes. "Just tell me what to do," she said. She was ready to engage.

Together, we created several different versions of a plan for her career transition. First, we explored her flower shop idea. After some research, I found that the average cost for launching a flower shop runs about $100,000 in her city. I told Brenda that in my opinion, it wasn't something that could happen soon. However, that didn't mean it was off the table.

"How would you feel," I asked her, "if this happened in twenty years? That's the time it would take to finance this idea while still pursuing your other goals. Would you be okay with that timeline?" She was game, so we proceeded to build a plan around saving for the cost of launching the flower shop.

Next, we tackled her proposed segue into a new career as a business coach. We talked through all the different options for how this profession might look and discussed what she'd need to do in terms of building her skillset, while making incremental moves toward a business coaching career.

After brainstorming several options, we found a plan

Brenda felt good about committing to. She would work on segueing into a development role with her current employer, in order to beef up her coaching expertise while still making the same salary she had today. This would allow her to not only keep saving money for her eventual exit but also build skill and experience that would be foundational to starting her own business. We even created an incremental plan for her to begin taking on coaching clients as a side business. We also built the flower shop saving strategy into her plan so that, down the road, she'd have the funds she needed to make that dream a reality.

Brenda is a very good example of where these derailers can prevent executives from living life on their terms, and by identifying them and having a plan for them, you can live the life you want. She's living proof that hope springs from taking action. Because cash flow management was a challenge for her, we created a budget with Brenda that keeps her spending in check. At the end of the month, she has extra money to put aside. The bonus she gets every year is now earmarked specifically for different goals, instead of being used for living expenses or paying down debt. Last time we met, she said to me, "This is awesome. I feel so good knowing that my budget totally works." She feels empowered, positive, and in control.

For me, it's just as rewarding to see Brenda making real progress. I helped her think about what was important to her and put together a manageable series of steps, but she's the one doing the work. This is her life, after all. I'm the facilitator, but the progress is her own. Today, thanks to her own engagement and commitment, she is well on her way to reaching her goals.

LYDIA'S STORY: HOPE BEGINS WITH INCREMENTAL ACTION

Lydia has owned and run a high-powered law firm for several decades. When we engaged, she had very little saved for retirement, knew she was behind, and wanted a plan that would help her get on track.

However, even though she knew she needed to make some big changes, she was initially slow to engage with the process. I tried to put together her plan, but she wouldn't return my phone calls or fulfill tasks I set for her on a timely basis. Despite wanting to help her get a plan together for retirement, there wasn't much I could do without her cooperation. After all, this was her life, not mine.

THE POWER OF A BUSINESS COACH

Lydia was referred to me by her business coach. I love hearing from a business coach, because I know that that person is working on their business and career already. The career is such a huge driver of them creating the life they want. Managing your career is absolutely critical to living life on your terms. Once they're already trying to do that on the business side, a financial expert can convert that business success into financial success. In Lydia's case, as with most of my clients, her business coach remains one of her most important trusted advisors, and one with whom we collaborate closely for our client's business and career success. We'll talk more about the value of engaging a business coach as part of your support network in Chapter 5.

Looking at her circumstances, it was easy to see why Lydia was slow to engage. Not only was she really busy, but she was not terribly sure that planning would make a difference for her.

I realized that I had to change my approach with Lydia. In order for her to engage, she had to experience hope that positive change was possible. We began meeting together every quarter for a frank discussion about where she stood financially. For people like Lydia who run their own company, having a budget is critical, but it can be difficult to separate business expenses from personal expenses. She needed constant communication in order to stay on track. In addition to Lydia's business coach, I brought together an awesome team of financial experts to offer the support she needed—a CPA, a bookkeeper, and an actuary.

Eventually, we got the plan done and started to implement it. Just as I anticipated, when Lydia started to see progress, she became a lot more excited and motivated. We put in place a retirement plan that lowers her taxable income and allows her to put away money in savings. Her consistency is paying off—she has saved nearly $300,000 over the past two years. When she had a bad six months because revenue lagged her expectations, she got a little behind in her finances. In the past, this would have constituted a major setback, but this time, having a plan let her take it in stride. Lydia knows the power of having a team that is working together for you—it's her secret weapon.

Following her plan is a lot of work, but Lydia is thrilled at how far she's come. She can see the progress she's making in real time. She feels wonderfully supported by the team we've put together to help her achieve her goals. It's made a real difference not only to her financial stability but to her mental well-being. She has confidence in taking on the challenges that come with running her own company. She knows that when the day comes for her to stop working, she can pull the trigger with confidence, knowing that she has enough money to live life on her own terms.

Lydia has come a long way from the procrastination and hopelessness she started with—today, she is a fabulous advocate for financial management. At a recent speaking engagement of mine, Lydia introduced me to the audience by saying, "I have to tell you, this approach to finances has been life changing for me."

FAILURES IN TRADITIONAL PLANNING

When you walk into a session with a traditional financial planner, you can almost guarantee that the first question they will ask you is, "When do you want to retire?" They'll work with you to pick a retirement day in the future, then go about figuring out how to invest your money. Then, when your last day of work comes, you can flip the switch, walk off into the sunset, and draw on your portfolio while never having to work again.

That future-oriented planning serves a purpose, but it misses the central question: what exactly do you want your life to look like? Important details like where you want to live, whether you want to downsize or upgrade your lifestyle, and how you'd like to spend your time once you leave your full-time career are almost never discussed by financial planners. For that matter, few of their clients have even spent the time thinking through those questions. As a result, even if they reach retirement with all the money they could want, they find themselves feeling unsatisfied without knowing why.

The financial planning industry seems to assume that everyone dreams of living the exact same life. It's as if no one in the industry has ever sat down and talked with a client, much less a woman executive client. Take a group of five different women at random, and you'll hear five different descriptions of what an ideal life looks like. Nobody in the industry is focusing on this—they're more focused on having money for the future.

Money is important, but it's important as a tool for living the life you want. Success isn't measured simply by how large your portfolio is, or whether you've maximized your retirement contributions. Success is measured by the quality of the life you are leading today. Your future planning plays a role in that quality of life, of course, but only if that future takes into account the goals, wants, needs, and passions that make your life different from everyone else's.

NO CONSIDERATION FOR UNIQUE NEEDS

Traditional financial planning is the one place where it's a mistake to treat men and women as equals. Women executives face unique financial issues different from men in the same positions. When the financial planning industry fails to consider those issues, it does women clients a major disservice.

For example, the industry does not consider the fact that the average woman, if she retires in her early sixties, will live thirty years in retirement, longer than the average man. It doesn't consider that most women will be single for the majority of those post-career years, or the higher cost of women's healthcare, both of which greatly impact quality of life during retirement.

The industry also fails to take into account the myriad challenges women face in business. Traditional planners may argue that career challenges are outside their purview; however, those challenges make a big difference in how well a woman is able to fund the life she wants, and how she defines quality of life for herself.

One of my clients is getting married soon. Because she is close to forty years old, she and her fiancé plan to start having children right away. The two of us have spent a lot of time discussing how marriage and family will impact not only her bills but her ability to earn money. During our meetings, we went over strategies she can deploy to overcome the challenges to her earning potential. She took those strategies into a negotiation with her workplace about flexibility. As a result, she scored a major victory for her quality of life: she now has the option to work from home as needed. In the long run, this flexibility is going to make a big impact on her ability to provide for her family while living the life she wants. It will allow her to take care of her children while still maintaining her career.

This is just one example of what it means to plan around the unique financial issues women face. When a planner doesn't take your unique circumstances into account—your goals, your needs, your day-to-day challenges—it may mean sacrificing your ability to live life on your terms. The traditional financial industry's limitations sometimes mean that people don't realize they've made these sacrifices until it's too late.

I was talking to a couple recently who said they were making sure to save money for retirement but didn't know if it was enough. As it turned out, they hadn't even had the conversation about when they wanted to retire. It came out in our conversation that the husband has a mandatory retirement age at his company of sixty-two; his wife didn't even know that. She said, "If he retires at sixty-two, why would I want to keep working?" Despite having worked with a financial planner for some years, they never had these discussions before they came to me.

Financial success is so much more than simply having a

given amount of money in a portfolio. It's about having the freedom to spend your time in a way that makes you happy. It's about achieving the things that are important to you.

A DIFFERENT APPROACH

At my firm, I've developed a very clear financial planning process focused on the four main derailers of women's financial success. As Lydia's and Brenda's stories show, this process makes all the difference to my clients. It's the integral piece of financial planning that will make or break your quality of life. It's the difference between working as though you're on a treadmill, trying to keep up with your expenses, and working on your own terms, empowered with full control of where your money is going.

Every plan I make is customized based on what an individual client wants. When I create a plan, I'm not telling the client what she's going to do. Instead, I'm drawing her out about what's important to her, guiding her in focusing those values into tangible goals, and helping her prioritize and plan around those goals. It's a give-and-take discussion that puts the client in charge of her own decisions. By the time I break her plan into actionable steps, she is ready to take action. It's a lot easier to follow a plan when you know it has been built on your terms.

Choice is the heart of the whole financial planning process I offer. My job is to create awareness and come up with solutions, but the client gets to choose. It's her life, her money, her job, her family—she should be the one to choose what's most important in her plan. Putting choice back in the client's hands makes her more engaged. She understands every step involved in taking her plan from dream to reality and understands that it's up to her to take those steps.

Another unique feature in my approach to planning is the resource component. I help my clients craft a customized team that can advise them on all the moving parts involved in a tailored financial plan. Depending on that client's goals and needs for support, I bring in people who are experts in career coaching, estate planning, accounting, business law, and whatever experts we have identified that will help the client reach her goals.

A client once likened me to the conductor of the orchestra—I'm an expert in designing the big-picture strategy and bringing together the best-qualified people to play each part. My goal is to make sure they are all taken care of by the best team possible.

I've found that this emphasis on collaboration is immensely appealing to women executives. Women have a natural tendency toward empathy, compassion, and emotional connection in their careers. We feel stronger and more secure in a collaborative environment than in trying to do everything alone. Even women in leadership tend to gravitate toward collaboration over flying solo.

This is the reason behind another important aspect of my approach to financial planning. I design all my clients' plans around incremental change. It allows for progress at each woman's own pace and comfort level.

It can't be denied that financial planning takes time and effort, two precious commodities in a woman executive's life. It can be hard for my clients to take that time away from their families, their careers, or their personal lives— it feels like just one more thing for them to do. That's why I make sure that their plan is designed to be accomplished one small piece at a time. Rather than impose a huge life change that would only overwhelm them, we set clear priorities and manageable goals, then chip away at them steadily.

This approach is more than just a philosophy. Where most traditional financial planners compile an eighty-page master document that they present to clients, I distill everything my clients need into a one-page plan summary. It takes all of our conversations about their goals into a simple outline, including where they currently are, where they want to be, the gaps in-between, and the incremental steps for bridging those gaps. It's everything they need to know to start making progress toward their best life, with all the potentially overwhelming details filtered out.

I started using this one-page summary because I knew from experience what clients do with the eighty-page summary: they get home, stick it in a drawer, and avoid it. By contrast, a one-page plan makes the whole financial planning process seem doable. It keeps the confusing details out of the picture to know what they have to do to get where they want to be, which is all they want to have to think about. Each meeting I have with the client, we update this one-page summary together based on the actions they've taken and the milestones they've achieved. It keeps them focused, on track, and lets them see their progress in real time.

QUALITY OF LIFE IS INTEGRAL

I can't say enough about how important it is that everything in this planning process is about what that woman executive wants her life to be. The entire planning process is constructed around how that person defines quality of life. Every step in the plan we create is tailored to help that client live life on her terms. Throughout the process of implementing the plan, she has the assurance that her efforts are yielding the life she wants for herself.

THE PROCESS

The process I'm going to guide you through in this book is based on overcoming the four major derailers we discussed in the Introduction. It starts with understanding where you want to go, i.e., your goals for your life. We won't even talk about numbers or money until further on in our process. Instead, we'll spend time exploring what is important to you in life personally, professionally, and financially.

Once those values have been laid out, we'll dig into the details. We'll find out exactly what's involved in sending your kids to college, paying off your home or buying a new home, growing your business or getting a leadership role in your industry, both from a numbers standpoint and a time-frame standpoint. We'll talk about the different options available for achieving these goals, examine how each option would affect the bigger picture of your life, and decide which plan feels the best to you.

The next step is getting a good picture of where you are right now with regard to your finances. We'll dive into a comprehensive analysis of your life today, looking at everything from your homeowner's insurance and risk management, to the investments you hold and the contributions you're making to your 401(k). We'll have a clear picture of where you are financially right now.

Once we know where you want to be and where you are currently, we can identify the gaps in-between and come up with solutions. Typically, there are at least a few options for bridging each gap, so we'll try on different scenarios for size and see which one feels like the best fit for you. Once we know what is important to you and what you're willing to do, given what we have to work with, we can come up with the action plan.

INTROSPECTION INTO YOUR BEST LIFE

This process works, but it can't happen without some deep introspection into your best life. Derailer number one, which we'll discuss in detail in Chapter 3, concerns the fact that most women executives never take the time to articulate—even in their own minds—what they want their life to look like.

I can't tell you how many people sit down in my office and immediately lay out exactly how much money they have in their 401(k) accounts. I understand why they do it—for the vast majority of people, financial planning means one thing: numbers.

Instead of numbers, though, I prompt them to think about living life. Helping them consider their passions and pursuits forces them to think outside of vague future concepts and instead reflect on the specifics of how they want their life to look in one year, three years, five years, ten years.

For some clients, thinking this way presents a real challenge. They might not have given themselves permission to think about their ideal life in years, even decades. They go to work, get a paycheck, and try to save money for retirement. They haven't been given a chance to sit back and say, "What *does* my dream life look like?"

On the other hand, there also are clients who have incredibly (sometimes unrealistically) lofty goals for their lives, given where they are starting from. But that doesn't mean I can't help them. It simply means they have a disconnect between the way they live now and what it will take to get to where they want to be. They know where they want to be, but they haven't yet grasped that without a plan, their future will be the same as their present. Until they know where they want to go, they will remain stuck on that treadmill.

I love seeing the change that comes over my clients when they discover the power of having goals and a plan to achieve them. Identifying their best life motivates them to follow the plan and engage with the process. Once they do that, they are amazed by how empowered and positive they feel. It's so much more than numbers. It's a holistic life satisfaction that they never thought they could have.

It allows them to transition to jobs that give them more satisfaction. It empowers them to live in places that make them happy to wake up in the morning. It gives them courage to make the kind of changes they have longed for.

I have experienced this kind of transformation in my own life, thanks to the same strategic financial planning principles I use with my clients. I want everyone to have the same opportunity I've had to do something they love, to benefit from hard work, and to enjoy quality of life.

Once you've specified your passions and pursuits, the next step is analyzing your current financial situation. The cornerstone of this step is taking a deep dive into cash flow management, the solution to derailer number two.

The analysis starts with a balance sheet, which lists your assets, liabilities, and net worth. A balance sheet is essentially a snapshot in time that tells you exactly what your life looks like in terms of finance, in this moment. There's no judgment around it—it's simply an accurate picture that allows you to know your financial health right now.

Next, you'll assess where your money is going every month. In addition to tracking expenditures, you'll also go through all insurance documents, estate plans, retirement options, tax returns, and every investment account you have. All this work yields a crystal-clear picture of where you are financially.

Following your financial analysis, we'll explore strategy around the source of your money, i.e., your career. The way you make money is, after all, a major component in your quality of life, and not just with regard to the amount you earn. The ways in which your job contributes to (or detracts from) your life as a whole must be considered alongside the financial benefits it brings. Both are equally important.

At this stage in the process, you'll come back to your passions and pursuits to ask more detailed questions around your career. In a perfect world, is this the job you'd like to be doing? Do you want to stay in the same industry until you retire? Do you want to climb the ladder, and if so, do you want to be the CEO or director of marketing? Do you want to sell your business someday, and if so, when do you envision doing that? All in all, what do you want out of your career?

Whatever your ultimate professional goals might be, achieving them starts with asking these important questions and comparing them against where you are now. This part of the process will help you identify the gaps between the career you want and the career you currently have, and understand the tools you can use, and the changes you need to make, in order to start working on your own terms.

The next step in the process is strategically leveraging traditional financial solutions. One area where traditional financial planning gets it right is in optimizing your tax situation and aligning your best investment strategy with your goals.

However, just as there is no one-size-fits-all solution for financial planning, there is no one-size-fits-all way to approach tax and investments. Every woman's best tax strategy depends entirely on her individual life, and her investments chosen should be based on her personal goals. Your current finances as well as your future goals determine what the best business structure might be for your company, the right accounts for allocating your resources, and the precautions you need to minimize liability and risk. As for investments, they should be smart, tax-efficient and inexpensive strategies that are in line with your goals and your comfort with risk.

CREATING A TAILORED PLAN

Once you've thought through everything that is important to you, designated your goals, analyzed your starting point, and created a plan of action for incremental change, it's time to put your plan into action. As you'll see in Chapter 7, the crucial first step of implementation is putting your plan in writing. Not only will having a written plan make your chances of success exponentially greater, but it also ensures that if your goals shift or life throws you a curveball, you'll be able to seamlessly build those changes into your plan without losing your momentum.

This is another area where traditional financial planning fails clients. It's rare that financial plans are designed to be flexible around possible changes in a client's life, goals, or circumstances. However, planners seldom (if ever) check in with their clients to see how the plan they've created is working in practice. As a result, when the client's life takes an unexpected turn—as life so often does—the plan goes out the window, and the client is back where they started.

After spending so much time and energy on creating a plan, the last thing I want is for you to lose accountability and focus. As a planner, I find it essential to circle back with each client at least once per year, if not more often. I remind them of what we set out to do and check in on how things are going for them.

You can and should do the same thing as you work through the plan you've created. By having a one-page plan summary that includes a clear list of action items, you'll be able to efficiently gauge your progress against your plan, and if your dream life has changed in the meantime, make any adjustments that are needed. The plan isn't meant to be set in stone; rather, it's a roadmap that continually evolves with your needs, goals, and circumstances. The key is to always have a plan that is relevant to your life, one that allows you to stay focused on your dreams and engaged in the process of achieving them.

SUPPORT YOUR JOURNEY

Ever since I started in this industry, I've been struck by how much value women find from coming together with a group of like-minded professional peers. High-achieving women have so much to share with each other on the key contributors to quality of life.

To support my clients in this area, I host an event every few months where I invite a dozen or so women executives to socialize, have discussions, and listen to an expert speak on a topic that can help them personally or professionally. I keep these gatherings small so that everyone involved can participate, both in the topic and in conversation with each other.

Over time, this gathering has become not just a place for education, but also a place for women executives to make meaningful connections. At these events, women professionals can finally let their guard down a little, enjoy a glass of wine, and be real about their lives with women who understand what it's like to live at their level. It's as much about making friends as it is about finding collaborative resources. It provides an opportunity for women to get to know each other better as professionals but also simply as people.

As high-achieving women, we need a good excuse to give ourselves the benefits of a supportive community. We'll talk in Chapter 8 about how you can find a collaborative community of your own, and how it will contribute to your overall quality of life.

MY ENCOURAGEMENT FOR YOU

If you're reading this book, you are likely in the unique and lucky position of having a good career that enables you to create your best life. If you're feeling unfulfilled, though, be assured that you can leverage your current situation to live the life you want. All you have to do is spend some time thinking about what that life looks like, and then put a plan together to make it a reality.

Planning can truly set you on a course to unlocking the life you dream of. If you identify it, plan for it, and pursue it, your hope of your best life will come to fruition.

I know it can seem like a lot, maybe more than you have time for. It's imperative to access your inherent courage—the courage that got you this far in your career—to embark on this journey to financial well-being. Rest assured, you don't have to have it all figured out right now. Your success starts with being open to the premise of planning and having the courage to act on your plan when the time comes. Remember, action is the source from which hope springs.

Your career and the income that comes with it are tools for achieving the life you want. All you need is to figure out how to make them work for you, instead of you working for them. Learning how to leverage your resources in the best possible way is what allows you to live your best life, not just in the future but right now, in the present.

Even though I work with women at the highest levels of their industry, I find over and over that women executives are often anxious about even having a conversation about personal finance. They're ashamed of where they are; they think they're supposed to be in a better place, that they should have accomplished more, that they will be judged for needing support. They've achieved so much, yet they're not always as happy as they feel they should be.

If that's where you find yourself as you begin this book, let me remind you of something: high-achieving women like you have undeniable courage. You're not afraid to take on powerful people and confront immense obstacles to get where you want to go. I encourage you to access that inherent courage and embark on this journey of financial well-being.

If there's one thing I can give you right now, as you embark on this journey, it would be a sense of hope. You can confidently follow these steps taught in the coming chapters, knowing that they will lead you to a better place. You absolutely are able to make progress toward living the life you want. All you have to do is follow the steps.

The next two sections of this book will guide you through the concrete actions of making progress toward living the life you want. This content is organized around laying out the four major derailers, the areas where we see the biggest issues and impediments to women executives' financial success. Some of these areas you may already have under control. Not everyone will have a cash flow problem; not everyone will feel like they need help managing their career. This book will help you improve your success in those areas, and, more importantly, help you see how those parts of the process fit together with the places of the process where you do need support.

One thing I can promise you is that this information will not be overwhelming. It is all designed to be incremental, manageable, and practical. Living your best life starts with the process of learning how to do it. We're going to do this together.

PART II

BUILDING YOUR BEST LIFE

SOLUTIONS FOR OVERCOMING THE MAJOR DERAILERS

In the next few chapters, you'll explore three of the major financial derailers in-depth. You'll see how those derailers stand between you and your dream life and discover unique, tailor-made solutions for approaching and overcoming them.

CHAPTER THREE

PASSIONS AND PURSUITS

OVERCOMING DERAILER ONE: ENSURING GOAL CLARITY

The first of the four major derailers concerns not knowing what you want personally, professionally, and financially. Accordingly, the first step of the planning process, the driver of all your success, is deep consideration of your personal, professional, and financial goals, i.e., your passions and pursuits. In this chapter, we'll walk through the process of envisioning your ideal life, starting with the big picture, then thinking through the details and prioritizing your goals over the course of one, three, and ten years. Your focus at this stage should be on what is possible and desirable.

MARIA'S STORY: BUILDING A LIFE ON YOUR TERMS, STEP BY STEP

Maria and I started working together at a time when she was ready to move on from her high-earning attorney job. However, it's hard for her to leave an industry where she makes such good money. Moreover, it's what she knows—her expertise in this industry is what makes her so very employable. At first, the answer seemed simple: she just needed to switch into another setting. She considered several options including moving to a different firm and working as in-house counsel at a corporation. Ultimately, after several interviews, she relocated to another city and joined a publicly held company as their in-house attorney.

While some things about her new situation were different, a lot has stayed the same. Practicing law is a demanding job, no matter what. Moreover, the company where she works is a start-up, where long days are part of the culture. The demands were taking a toll on Maria's personal life. Her health was suffering. She was truly not happy.

Maria ultimately realized that, while she makes good money in the legal industry, she can only keep pace with it for so long. Fortunately, over the years that we've been working together, Maria has proved to be good at following her plan. With a focus on saving as much money as possible, she and her husband have been monitoring their cash flow, maxing out their 401(k), executing stock options, and leading a modest lifestyle with no complaints. All that dedication has paid off tremendously. In fact, if Maria stopped saving today, she'd be just fine. Her plan and her commitment to it are that good.

After many years, Maria has nearly arrived at the long-awaited point where she can quit her job and transition to a career that is much closer to her heart: the nonprofit sector. It will involve lowering her cost of living even more, but she is more than willing to make that sacrifice in order to have a better quality of life. After years of preparing financially, she is now set to make this leap.

In telling Maria's story, it's important for me to note that she wasn't always ready to make that sacrifice. It has been an evolution over many years. She came to me wanting a change in her career, but she was not quite ready to give up the income benefits that her career offered. Little by little, we tailored her financial plan to make incremental shifts that helped her realign her lifestyle with a more modest income. She also spent a lot of time thinking through what was important to her. Ultimately, she found herself wanting a meaningful job and a better quality of life more than she wanted the income.

In a way, Maria has been living life on her terms since the moment she and I began working together. The incremental approach focused around her passions and pursuits allowed her to make changes thoughtfully and intentionally and to try different solutions until she found the one that felt right for her. In the end, she felt completely ready to make this change into a lower-paying industry because she's been planning it for a long time. Moreover, she has established habits that will support her in making this change. She keeps track of where her money goes. She knows how to save. These habits will allow Maria and her husband to live life on their own terms.

PASSIONS AND PURSUITS

The first big step in financial planning is examining your passions and pursuits. Passions are the interests you feel deeply about, such as taking a month out of every year to travel or having more time to spend with your family. Pursuits are your particular goals or endeavors that you are committed to, such as paying for your child's college education, or saving for the down payment on a house. Passions represent the big picture of your ideal life; pursuits are the individual, concrete components of that life. Considering these two elements of your dream life kicks off the process of comprehensive exploration and analysis of your current situation and desired future.

Both passions and pursuits are fundamental to having goal clarity. Not having that goal clarity is the first derailer for women executives. After all, if you don't know what you're planning for, you can't make good plans. By contrast, when you have those passions and pursuits clearly articulated, they determine the direction you are aiming for as you set your course. Capturing the key elements of your ideal life drives your entire planning process forward.

Everyone is an individual; your passions and pursuits will differ from anyone else's. Moreover, people's passions and pursuits do have a tendency to shift over time. Any changes in a client's life could mean that their ideal life is taking a new shape. In order to achieve it, we need to always be clear on what their goals are and make sure their plan is on track.

For example, one of my clients announced to me that she was getting married. This was great news, and I was very happy for her, but I also had to let her know that this new goal would change the shape of her financial plan and all the other goals it contained. Adding in a spouse meant that we needed to consider his goals, his financial situation, and how they would combine these goals and resources to live life together. The couple also had to balance their overall quality of life goals against their goals for the wedding they were planning.

This conversation was a crucial part of helping my client ensure her happiness going into marriage. By talking about this specific goal ahead of time, she could make decisions that aligned well with her other life goals and contributed to her overall vision for her future.

Another good example is the couple I met with recently, who told me they wanted to help their two children with college. This was of great personal importance to both of them, since neither of them had any financial support for their education. Forced to independently finance their college careers, both of them finished school with sizeable student loans.

That debt had taken its toll in more ways than one. They had actually put off having children until it was paid down. Now, with two children on the verge of going to college, they wanted very much to save their children some of the struggle they had endured as a result of their education debt.

I empathized with their desire to provide for their children. At the same time, I tend to be a firm believer in not sacrificing your own financial future for the well-being of others. My role was not to tell them what to do but to help them see the outcome of their possible choices. I presented several different financial options for them, within several different school tuition levels, and showed how paying more versus less would impact their lifestyle once they reached retirement. It was a tough conversation, one that forced them to think hard about what is important to them. Ultimately, it allowed them to consider their emotional desires against practical realities and make a choice that felt right for them.

There isn't a right or wrong answer when it comes to goal clarity. It's simply a matter of asking the questions about what is really important to you within that goal, understanding it in relation to where you are now, and deciding what you are willing to allocate to that goal.

It's easy to get caught up in life events, good or bad, and forget that you have choices. A big part of my job is simply reminding my clients that they do have choices. With every decision we make, there's a give and take. I'm thrilled when they bring me into that process; I love the look on their faces when they clearly see the path to accomplishing what is genuinely important to them.

IDENTIFYING YOUR OWN PASSIONS AND PURSUITS

Identifying your passions and pursuits starts with considering the macro view of your life. First, you'll consider where you are personally, professionally, and financially. These are the areas that together determine your entire quality of life, and you'll use your understanding of the way they look now as a launch pad for imagining how those areas could be better. If, like some of my clients, it feels like too much to consider, just narrow it down to your top three goals. In a perfect world, what would you like your life to look like personally, professionally, and financially? Consider how you would like each of those areas to look both now and in the future.

Once you've spent some time on the big picture, you'll drill down into the details. Don't be afraid to get "granular." Forcing yourself to really consider the financial implications will help you with the next step—putting these goals in order of priority.

IMAGINE YOUR IDEAL LIFE

I've included a worksheet in the Appendix that will help you articulate your passions and pursuits. For now, here are just a few of the questions I lead clients through in imagining different areas of their ideal life, from the big-picture concepts to the details that really flesh out a goal:

- Would you like to move to another city? Which one? When would you like this move to happen? How much does a house cost in that area?
- Do you want to buy a house, or a boat, or a vacation home? How much would you want to spend on it each month? When would you want to buy it? When and how often would you plan to use it?
- Do you want to have children? How many? When do you want to have them? Do you plan on sending them to private school? Do you want to pay for their college education?

The next step is to put these goals in order of priority. I find that in many cases, clients need to choose which goals are most important to them. While it doesn't mean they are not all possible, it's true that they are often not all possible right now.

Ask yourself, if you could pick only one or two goals to accomplish within each area of your life in the next three, five, or ten years, which goals would they be? This is a crucial part of the process when it comes to making decisions aligned with what is most important to you.

Once you've set your priorities, pick some milestones that indicate progress toward those goals. Where would you like to be three years from now, in regard to your career, your personal life, and your finances? What about in five years, or ten? In other words, what would have to happen between now and the next ten years for you to feel like you're well on your way to achieving the dream life you've envisioned?

Finally, you'll write out your definition of success in each area. The answer is different for everyone. For example, some people will feel successful if they make more money in five years than they do now. But for others, like Maria, success means making less money but having more time to devote to her family and spending less time at work. Maybe for you, success means something as simple as being able to cook dinner for your family on a regular basis. Any answer is fine—the important thing is that you write down whatever feels authentic to you.

You may wonder how these simple, mundane goals relate to finances. The truth is that how you manage your money enables or undercuts your ability to reach your goals. I had one set of clients tell me that they defined success in terms of a happy family, enjoyable career, and a stress-free retirement. The more we talked, the more detail they offered on what those goals meant to them. They kept coming back to less stress in each area of their lives.

As we talked, it was clear that the stress they experienced came from not intentionally managing their money. They worked hard and saved nearly everything they earned but had not spent much time tracking their finances. While they thought they were probably okay, they didn't know it for a fact.

Not knowing about their money was causing stress, and that stress was getting in the way of a happy family life, an enjoyable career, and confidence about retirement. They were saving all their money instead of spending it on family vacations. Their financial uncertainty was affecting their ability to enjoy their careers. They didn't know where their finances stood in relation to the prospect of retirement. As a result, they weren't permitting themselves to live the life they want, out of fear and uncertainty.

As we talked, we used their definition of success to refine their big-picture goals, then drill down into the details. We talked about the reality of how much it costs to go to college, something they had never researched. We talked about putting money to work towards their goals better, rather than having it sit in a savings account. I love seeing the fear and uncertainty on their faces change to relief and excitement as they begin to think about their goals with new clarity. I love asking the questions that help them make decisions that enable them to finally live a life that they love.

CHALLENGES FOR WOMEN

Most busy women executives have not considered their passions and pursuits in a very long time, certainly not in a systematic way like this. They are far too busy on the treadmill of their lives, dealing with too much on their plate, to give themselves the opportunity to think about their ideal life. They may know they're not happy where they are now, but they don't know what to do, so they do nothing until they get to a breaking point and say, "Something has to change." Needless to say, the last minute before you break is not a great time to be asking all these big questions.

STRESS TAKES ITS TOLL

All this stress about the present and uncertainty about the future takes its toll. It's far more common than it should be for highly successful women executives to have a problem with alcohol or even drugs. In fact, people who work more than fifty hours a week are three times more likely to abuse alcohol than those who work less. Outside of substance abuse, there are a tremendous number of women executives who are simply miserable in their careers, anxious in their personal lives, and too busy surviving from day to day to do anything about it. Clearly, changing quality of life can have a positive impact for many women execs.[12]

That's where the incremental approach becomes essential. I've learned to reassure my clients at the outset that they don't have to change everything overnight. While we make a big-picture plan, we pick one or two goals to focus on and remain flexible in how we prioritize those goals within their greater plan.

Once you begin considering your passions and pursuits, don't be surprised if you have a hard time getting specific. I've found that many women executives at the outset of their planning process tend to list vague, incomplete, and amorphous goals. It can be hard to shift perspective from the immediate to the ideal.

12   http://interventionstrategies.com/17-statistics-on-drug-abuse-among-lawyers/

There's also a tendency to start timidly generating very small-scale goals that are only expressed in terms of numbers, e.g., needing this much for retirement or this much to pay off their mortgage.

We have found that for high earners, there can be a tendency to overestimate their ability to fund these goals. Because they really don't know where they stand financially, they don't realize what they can and can't afford, without planning.

This can make it very challenging in the beginning when we start to work together. They think that because they make so much money, they should be able to fund everything they want without any planning or making any hard decisions.

I have to help them see that while they're making a lot of money, they're also spending it in a way that undercuts their future goals. To achieve their ideal life, they must begin by training themselves to spend money differently. Until they are able to retrain their spending habits, they won't be able to live the life they want.

Retraining is not something that happens right away. It only happens if a client is engaged and ready to put in the work. For some clients, that commitment is a long time coming. I can't do it for them. But when they come back understanding that it will be a process and they're ready to commit to the work, the progress they make is truly awesome.

THE KEY TO SUCCESS

Being successful at designing your own passions and pursuits takes time. You need to stretch yourself to dream big. Remember, your goals are unique to you—your ideal life is not meant to be a one-size-fits-all solution.

At this stage in the process, you're not worrying about what seems doable. Instead, you're meant to dwell on your desires. Naturally, you will inevitably have to make choices, prioritize, and engage in give-and-take around your goals. For now, though, specificity is the goal. By being specific and digging into the details of your dream life, you improve the likelihood of success in achieving the plans you make.

Successful planning requires you to be cognizant that you will most likely need to make choices about what is most important to you and what you are willing to give up. You also can't have everything you want by tomorrow. But that's okay. By doing the work of reflection and putting together a plan that you work through incrementally, you will achieve these milestones. And I can promise you that it will be even more exciting than you imagine. Along the way, you'll experience your progress, which is also exciting. Every intentional choice you make enables the next one.

Through good planning and committed implementation, life on your terms is within your reach. As you consider your passions and pursuits, don't hold back—a good plan starts with an honest look at what is really important to you. You are in a unique place where you can create your ideal life. Don't be afraid to dream big.

PASSIONS AND PURSUITS: KNOWING WHAT IS IMPORTANT TO YOU ALLOWS YOU TO PUT TOGETHER A PLAN OF ACTION

- Spend time thinking about your ideal life, what is important to you personally, professionally, and financially.
- Put details to your goals.
- Prioritize the goals in terms of importance to you and when they need to happen.
- Know that your goals will evolve, and you will often need to make choices.

CHAPTER FOUR

CASH FLOW MANAGEMENT

OVERCOMING DERAILER NUMBER TWO—TAKING CONTROL OF CASH FLOW MANAGEMENT

High earners know how to spend money but often do not know where it goes. This chapter is focused on identifying where your money is going and directing it in a way that accords with the goals you uncovered in the exploration of your passions and pursuits.

Consideration of cash flow management arises out of the exercise of analyzing your current situation to generate a snapshot of your financial life. This exercise is essential because it provides a way to compare your current financial situation to your passions and pursuits and identify gaps where there is insufficient money to fund your goals. We'll start with an overview of this cash flow analysis, then outline the specific strategies you can use for tracking spending and developing a workable budget that aligns with your goals.

JENNIFER'S STORY: FINDING THE PATTERNS IN YOUR SPENDING

A few months ago, I began meeting with Jennifer, a top-earning executive who is also a single mother. We sat down and began, as we always do, with talking about what was important to her, how her ideal life would look personally, professionally, and financially.

One of Jennifer's biggest desires that came up in that conversation was to have a sense of control and security about her finances. Despite having multiple sources of income—her generous paycheck, stock options, a regular bonus—she didn't have a firm grasp of where her money was going every month, and that feeling added a lot of stress to her life.

I gave her a spreadsheet with categories for income, fixed expenses, and discretionary expenses, and I asked her to write down how much she thought she spent in each category per month. After she was done, we counted up the amounts she'd entered and found that her sheet reflected a surplus.

Jennifer was surprised, but I was not. It's extremely common for women executives to have little idea of how much they spend on miscellaneous, impulsive purchases. In Jennifer's case, one of her accounts was consistently depleted because her expenses were out of control. Despite her good income, she found herself in the red and paying for things on credit cards every month.

We started to track Jennifer's expenses by linking her accounts to a financial tracking software that records and categorizes every single transaction. Credit cards, debit cards, direct deposits, automatic bill pay—every amount of money that went in or out of her account showed up on this software. For a couple of months, Jennifer and I both simply watched the cash flow in and out. We saw exactly where the money went.

I have found that it only takes about two months of tracking to see a pattern. In Jennifer's case, a lot of her income went toward supporting her son in not-strictly-necessary ways. The amount of money she spent every month on gym memberships, personal trainer fees, and other activities that she felt were helpful to his self-esteem were creating serious financial challenges for her.

Once we identified the big areas where her money was going, we talked about where she was willing to lower those expenses. Some areas were nonnegotiable, such as mortgage, car insurance, or utilities. Others, however, had room for give and take. I asked her, "What is a dollar amount that sounds good for groceries? How about for health and fitness? How about for dining out?" There was no right or wrong answer—it all came down to how she would like to spend the money she had left over from her fixed expenses. Together, we created a discretionary budget for how much she would spend on her house, on shopping for clothing, and on saving money for some of her future goals.

Just a few months later, Jennifer expressed incredible relief. She had never realized before how much of her general life stress came from not having a real grip on where her money was going. Managing her cash flow not only gave her clarity on the "missing money" in her accounts, but it allowed her to actually have a real surplus, one that she could earmark for the things she wanted, both in the long term and in the present moment.

KNOWING WHAT YOU'RE WORKING FOR

It's terrible to be always working yet feel as though it's never enough. When you already feel totally out of control, it can make for tremendous anxiety around tracking your cash flow. But through the awareness built by this exercise, you'll gain real hope that things can get better. Once you know where your money is going, you can choose to spend it differently. When you find the root of the problem, the hard part is over. Now you get to start making the exciting choices.

Creating a budget brings more than just financial benefits. It allows you to see how even a small effort at saving can make a difference with every month that goes by. You're not making more money or working harder; instead, you're making progress using money that you would have spent elsewhere—in many cases, not even in a meaningful place. Tracking your money's growth lets you feel the excitement and hope of making real headway toward your goals.

Naturally, every budget needs a little tinkering. You might try to cut your expenses in certain areas, then come back to it the next month knowing that life didn't feel as good. At that point, you rearrange some priorities, allocate new amounts to different categories, and see if it works better for you. Budgeting is a dynamic give and take, one that updates every day as you spend money.

Most of my clients use my tracking software to save for their specific goals and stay on track with their cash flow. Each month, if not every few days, they just check in and look at how their money has been moving. They might find they're getting close to overspending in one area, while they might find they have extra funds available in another.

Doing this isn't a chore—rather, it creates awareness so that they can make the best choices. It's not about making life less fun—it's about staying engaged in the process of living your best life.

WHAT'S IN THIS CHAPTER

In this chapter, I'm going to lead you through all the steps I take with my clients. First, I'll explain why managing cash flow is such a major derailer for women executives, and why addressing it makes such a big difference. Next, I'll show how cash flow management fits into the financial planning process. I'll provide a brief overview of how to conduct an analysis of your overall financial situation, but I promise not to overwhelm you with a lot of detail for that analysis. The goal in this chapter is to give you cash flow management solutions.

Finally, we'll take a deep dive into those solutions, which starts with tracking your own cash flow. I'm going to ask you to write down where you think you spend your money. Next, we're going to actually track it and see how your beliefs line up with the reality.

There are many ways you can track your spending. Some people prefer to use a smartphone app (such as those listed in the Appendix), while others prefer an old-fashioned Excel spreadsheet. Find a way that you're comfortable with, one that is easy for you to use so you can check in often.

As stated earlier, it only takes a couple of months of tracking to establish trends. Once those trends are visible, we'll go through the steps of creating and following a budget that works for you. We'll also take a second look at the goals informed by your passions and pursuits and put some numbers around them. This will allow you to see how you can actually fund them. You can make some choices as to how to reallocate your funds in a way that lets you save for those goals. By the end of the chapter, you'll have a firm grasp of where you spend your money and be empowered to redirect it in whatever way you choose.

WHY IS CASH FLOW MANAGEMENT SO IMPORTANT?

After years of working with high-earning women executives, I've found that their cash flow management problems are not a matter of not having enough money coming in. Instead, the problem is not knowing where it's going. Some of my high-earning clients are not terribly happy with their lives right now, so they get temporary gratification by spending money at will. They get a fleeting satisfaction from the things they buy; afterward, however, the money and the satisfaction are gone, and they are no closer to living life the way they want than they were before.

As it happens, these are usually the same clients who, like Jennifer, estimate their monthly expenses and come out with what looks like a surplus at the end, even when they came to me knowing that they are in the red. What this shows me is that they don't know where they are spending. Once these clients get a real grasp of where they are spending their money, they can choose to do it differently.

Awareness and management of cash flow is such a huge piece to financial planning, yet I've encountered few financial planners doing it for their clients. Admittedly, it is a time-consuming process, but I have found it to be tremendously successful for every woman executive I work with. By getting your cash flow under control and having a strategy around it, you can be assured of having the money you need to live the life you want.

THE DANGERS OF ENTITLEMENT

I have a client in San Francisco, one of the country's most expensive places to live. Together, she and her husband make a healthy income every year. Nevertheless, they are still renting an apartment because they can't afford to buy a home. A closer look at their finances revealed that their expenses are way out of line. They feel like there will always be more money, so why should they worry about spending a little extra here and there? But it doesn't help them save money, either for a house or (as this client recently informed me) for the $38,000 tuition bill for each of their two kids to attend preschool.

When you work hard, it's easy to feel justified in spending it in any way that feels good at the time. This doesn't only happen when you feel miserable with your job, your schedule, or life in general. It's true even in the good times, when you are making good money and expect there will always be more money on its way next month. But in either case, this kind of spending doesn't allow you to get any closer to funding the life you want.

Cash flow management brings awareness of how much your life costs and where the money is going. As an example, I have a client who is sixty years old now and would like to retire in seven years. After looking at her cash flow, I had a frank conversation with her about that timeline. It was clear that she had little understanding of what her current lifestyle costs. If she wanted to maintain her current lifestyle after retiring, she needed a much better awareness of the expenses involved in that standard of living.

Awareness is just as crucial for any other goal you might

want to fund, including a change of career. Think back to Maria, the woman attorney who wanted to leave law for nonprofit work. As an attorney, she made several hundred thousand dollars last year. The only way she can go from that into a job that earns a fraction of that salary is by shifting her lifestyle to a more modest range. Otherwise, she'll have a job she enjoys more, but her quality of life won't be any better.

Awareness around cash flow leads to control and change. Once a client knows the numbers behind the life they currently lead, they have the opportunity to make informed choices. This brings them tremendous hope because they're driving the process instead of being driven by the need to make more money. It's intentional and it empowers them. Now they actually feel like they have a plan that's going to work.

Cash flow also can shed light on what changes you might need to make to strategically manage your business or career. We'll dive more deeply into that aspect of planning in Chapter 5.

That is the best thing about cash flow management—the way it makes you feel. Life on a treadmill, always trying to keep up with the next bill, is no way to live. It feels like you have no hope for things to ever be different. By contrast, cash flow management gives you the freedom of choice in your life. It allows you to direct your money toward attaining the goals you've established, and it allows you to see progress and experience hope along the way.

HOW CASH FLOW MANAGEMENT FITS INTO THE OVERALL PROCESS

We started with asking what you want your dream life to look like, what your passions and pursuits are for today, identifying your needs, your dreams, your wishes and goals, personally, professionally, and financially. Once you have clarity around your passions and pursuits, the next step is to analyze where you are financially. The analysis gives a snapshot, a lay of the land, that reveals the gaps between the life you dream of living and your life as it stands today.

That analysis will show you whether certain goals have a lower probability of attainment, based on your current financial situation. It will identify gaps where there is insufficient money to fund goals, as well as opportunities for redirecting cash flow. Once you know what you have to work with, you can figure out what the solutions are.

AN OVERVIEW

When I'm creating a financial plan for a client, I don't start with training cash flow habits. First, I want a good picture of where that client is financially before any new habits have been formed. Understanding their income sources and how those sources are currently being used lets me gauge how realistic their goals are.

After I've talked with a client about what's really important to them, and they create a specific picture of what they would love their life to look like, we dive into the numbers. I help the client collect all the data relevant to their finances. (You can do the same with the detailed document checklist provided in the Appendix.) This checklist includes investment and savings accounts (retirement accounts, real estate, stock option details, etc.), income information (such as paystubs and tax returns), details on their debts (like mortgages, student loans, and car loans), and insurance policies.

Next, we use all of those numbers to create a balance sheet, which tells us their net worth. Net worth is that snapshot in time of your financial health. As a planner, I don't care what that number happens to be, even if it's negative. All I want at this stage is to know where that client stands financially.

DATE

Assets

Cash Accounts			
Savings	$ -		
Checking	$ -		
		$ -	
Taxable Accounts			
Brokerage Account	$ -		
Trust Account	$ -		
		$ -	
Retirement Assets			
401k Account	$ -		
IRA	$ -		
		$ -	
Life Insurance (cash value)			
Insurance Policy	$ -		
		$ -	
Residential Real Estate			
Home value	$ -		
		$ -	
Total Assets:		$ -	

Liabilities

Mortgage			
Mortgage terms (x%, due when)	$ -		
		$ -	
Additional Loans (Car, Student)			
Loan terms (x%, due when)	$ -		
		$ -	
Total Liabilities:		$ -	
NET WORTH		$ -	

To determine net worth, we write down all the client's assets on a balance sheet. Below the assets, we write down liabilities. Subtract liability from the assets, and this is your net worth.

Next, I have the client fill out a basic spreadsheet of expenses. Just like Jennifer in the story at the beginning of the chapter, this spreadsheet starts with listing the amount of your income you take home every month, after deductions. This is the amount of income you have to spend on life.

Next, you'll write down your fixed expenses—amounts that stay pretty much the same each month, such as your mortgage, utilities, car payment, school tuition for your kids, etc. Finally, you'll write down how much you estimate spending on various discretionary expenses each month—dining out, entertainment expenses, gym membership, shopping for yourself or your children, and so on.

The next step is diving into your investments. We look at everything you're invested in, the type of accounts you have, and we determine your asset allocation. For example, how much money do you have in growth investments, like stocks? How much do you have in what are considered traditionally safer investments, like fixed income or bonds? What are your investment choices in your 401(k) plan? We'll write down every account, noting how much money it contains, how it's being invested, and how we can minimize the taxes you pay on it. (We'll discuss taxes in more detail in Chapter 6.)

Next, we go over risk management, examining how well you are financially protected. We'll get into the specifics of how much homeowners insurance you need to have, or how much you should have for car insurance and life insurance. You can have an awesome investment portfolio, but if you wind up in a terrible accident—your house burns down, you have a significant medical emergency, etc.—having inadequate insurance could wipe out everything you've been working on. Just a couple basic things can make a tremendous difference if you don't have them.

Again, none of this assessment part has any judgment or change attached to it. We're not doing anything at this point except getting a full picture of where you are right now. Once we have that picture, we can begin making decisions about how to make certain changes that help you achieve the life you want.

MANAGING WHERE THE MONEY GOES

I recently asked women at a conference where I was speaking how many of them thought they knew where their money went. Only about a third of them said they did know. Most of the women in that room had no idea, not even a less-than-accurate one, of what happened to the money they made from one month to the next.

The purpose of the cash flow exercise in the previous section is to become aware of what you don't know. The next step is to find out where your money actually does go each month, and there are multiple options for doing that. You can use a budgeting app, a spreadsheet, or financial planning software—whatever way resonates best with you. All of these options will allow you to track your expenses.

PERSONAL CASH FLOW	Month	Month	Month
Net Income	$	$	$
Fixed Expenses			
Rent/Mortgage	$	$	$
Medical			
Groceries			
Homeowner Insurance			
Miscellaneous			
Utilities			
Phone/Internet/cable			
Gas			
Student Loans			
Garbage/Water			
Car Payment			
Childcare			
Home Maintenance			
TOTAL:			
Discretionary Budget			
Travel	$	$	$
Auto Service			
Cash/ATM			
Clothing			
Credit Cards			
Education			
Entertainment			
Health & Fitness			
Savings			
Dining Out			
Sports& Hobbies			
Kids			
Shopping			
Home			
Unclassified			
TOTAL:	$	$	$
Total Expenses:			
Surplus/Deficit			

Budgeting apps are easy to link to your bank account and credit cards. For many women executives, that's honestly the easiest way to do it. Once you've linked your account, every single transaction will show up and be categorized. For the first month or two, you'll simply watch the money going in and out, checking in several times per week—not to change anything, but simply to get in the habit of staying current with your cash flow. As you go, you can begin categorizing all the income and expenses. Again, you should reserve all judgment during these first couple of months. You're simply collecting data to understand where your money typically goes.

At the end of the first month, you'll write down the data about which categories your money flowed into. At the end of the second month, you'll do the same thing and compare the two months side by side. Your comparison should start with the two big categories: fixed expenses and discretionary spending.

Fixed expenses are the ones that you have to allocate money for every month. However, for some of them (like groceries or gas in your car), there is a degree of control over how much you have to spend. It's about awareness, and there may be an opportunity to cut some of these fixed expenses, which we'll get to in a moment. At this point, the first thing is to figure out how much you *have* to spend each month. After that, you'll have a clear idea of how much you have left to spend on the discretionary category.

Discretionary expenses are where you'll find the bulk of the changes you can make in your spending habits. This is the stuff that makes life fun but that you don't really need. Once you know where you tend to spend in the discretionary category, you can decide if you're willing to cut back on some of these expenses by whatever amount you pick.

Tracking your expenses will reveal if there actually is a surplus of money available for you to put toward your goals. If you've tracked your expenses and find that there is money left over, that's great! More often, though, people find that there isn't a surplus, even if there should be, because they've already spent it. That doesn't mean there couldn't be a surplus—it means that their current spending habits don't allow for one right now.

Creating a budget is just a matter of asking yourself how much you think you can cut from a given spending category, then testing that amount out. You may try a certain amount and find that it doesn't work for you. On the other hand, you may be able to do more. You don't know until you try it.

Sometimes, it's less a matter of how you spend your money, and more a matter of where. For example, one of my clients has only ever shopped for groceries at Whole Foods. As a result, her grocery bill was through the roof.

Groceries are certainly a fixed expense, but I reminded her that there were other places where she shops that would allow her to take home the same amount of food for her family without spending nearly as much money.

I asked her what she thought a reasonable number was to spend on groceries. She confessed that she had no idea; she had never thought about it before. Together, we settled on a number that was about 60 percent of what she was currently spending and agreed that she would see how far it could get her at a different store. It was a huge change and represented a whole new area of control over her finances that she didn't realize she could have.

CREATING A SUCCESSFUL BUDGET

The goal with creating a budget is to live within your means, so that you free up some of the money you're currently spending for use in funding your passions and pursuits. Once you are clear about your fixed expenses, you then get to decide how much discretionary money you are willing to allocate to funding a given goal.

Every single part of the financial planning process is about your personal choice. But choice begins with awareness. Cash flow is about awareness of what you have to work with, how you are currently spending it, and which things are more important to you than what you're spending money on right now.

Now, it's time to put a dollar amount behind the goals you've decided are important.

COMMON GOALS

Knowing how much to save is just one part of the budgeting process. Most people have many goals competing for their money, so determining where the money goes becomes a priority issue. There's only so much money, so how do we allocate it? There are rules of thumb we'll cover here regarding goals that have come up frequently with clients.

Common goals include children's education, shifting into a more fulfilling but less lucrative career, caring for aging parents, moving to a different city, spending more time traveling, and of course, retirement. Before you begin allocating any money to them, it's important to assess what each of these goals is likely to cost, and how that cost translates into an amount to set aside each month. That will give you a better understanding of how far your money will go in funding each goal, how much you need to earn to afford your lifestyle and fund your goals, and help you make decisions about which goals are most important to fund now, and which you can address down the road.

EMERGENCY FUND

This may not be on your radar at all. In fact, no client has ever come to me and said, "I would like to save money for an emergency fund." However, as a planner, the first thing I do for every single client is recommend an emergency savings account that's always there if the unexpected happens.

There are a couple of different ways to decide how much should go into an emergency fund. In my industry, people say you need between three and six months' worth of fixed expenses. However, if you're part of a couple and both of you work, I often suggest creating an emergency fund that contains the low end of the fixed expenses amount—maybe just three or four months' worth of fixed expenses. If one of you should lose their job, the other is still making money. However, if you live on a single income, I advise erring on the side of six months of fixed expenses.

Sometimes, I'll have a client whose quality of life is greatly enhanced by the sense of peace that comes with having a substantial amount of money in the emergency fund. Ultimately, the choice about this fund is very personal. There's an opportunity cost for keeping money attached to an emergency fund—after all, that money is not earning for you the way it would if it were being invested. I always advise clients that they lose about 2 percent of the value of that money every year, due to inflation. For my clients who have large emergency funds, I remind them that if they were to take some of that money and invest it in a sound portfolio, they would have some sort of a return. However, making a return is not the purpose of an emergency fund. Its purpose is to provide a safety net for the possibility of something happening outside your plan and for giving folks peace of mind.

CHILDREN'S EDUCATION

Many clients come to me saying that they would like to pay for four years of university education for their children. Very often, though, when we dig into what that would cost and how much money is available for that goal, they have to make concessions on that goal.

"Concession" doesn't mean that they cannot contribute anything to their child's education. Rather, they have to reexamine their priorities around this goal. While I utilize software to help clients with education planning, there are online calculators that show you how much college education costs. (Some good ones can be found in the Appendix.) A four-year private school looks very different than a four-year public school in terms of cost. Once a client is able to detail out what their ideal goal would look like, we parse out the costs associated with it and see how much they are able and willing to pay for the goal.

LONG-TERM CARE FOR PARENTS

Long-term care for parents is something I'm dealing with more and more. "Women who become caregivers for an elderly parent or friend are more than twice as likely to end up living in poverty than if they aren't caregivers," says Cindy Hounsell, president of the Women's Institute for a Secure Retirement (WISER).[13] If they take time off work, not only do they lose pay, but those lost wages can affect their Social Security, pension payouts, and other savings—threatening their future finances. Studies estimate that two out of three informal caregivers are women, many of whom are middle-aged mothers with children or adult children living in their households.[14]

The cost of putting a parent into professional assisted-living care can be daunting. MetLife says that kind of care averages about $42,000 a year. A private room in a nursing home averages more than $87,000.[15] But the cost of keeping a relative at home can be very high, too.[16]

BUYING A HOUSE

Buying a house comes down to detailing out what you want and when you want it. I usually suggest people put 20 percent down to avoid the added cost of mortgage insurance and in order to minimize their monthly pay-

13   Cindy Hounsell, "How to take care of aging parents and yourself." Fidelity Viewpoints, 9/27/17, https://www.fidelity.com/viewpoints/personal-finance/caring-for-aging-parents

14   14 "Women and Caregiving: Facts and Figures." Family Caregiver Alliance, https://www.caregiver.org/women-and-caregiving-facts-and-figures

15   Marilyn Geewax, "Discovering the Trust Cost of At-Home Caregiving," heard on NPR Morning Edition, May 1, 2012

16   https://www.aarp.org/caregiving/financial-legal/info-2017/long-term-care-calculator.html

ment. The decisions around this goal require knowing how much housing costs in your part of the country, what you would like to buy, and what you're able to buy given your financial situation right now. Bear in mind that the costs include more than just having the 20 percent down payment—there are other costs to consider.

COSTS TO CONSIDER IN BUYING A HOUSE

- How much you can realistically pay for a mortgage on a monthly basis
- The amount of property tax in your state
- The costs of maintenance of the house
- Insurance
- HOA fees
- The full cost of owning versus renting
- Your ability to pay the monthly mortgage payment from a cash flow perspective

VACATIONS

Vacations are a big goal for my clients. This expense isn't usually a big derailer in the cash flow management category, simply because it's not a regular expense. A one-time expense tends to be an easier thing for people to pay for. However, it is important to consider how deluxe a vacation you want in order to make progress in funding this goal.

It's also important to have a plan around paying for your vacation up-front, versus putting it on a credit card. This is one expense that often deserves its own savings goal throughout the year.

RETIREMENT

When it comes to retirement, determining your funding need starts with your cost of living. As a result, it's a goal where gender becomes a big issue. Because of the many financial challenges women have throughout life, retirement funding is one area that absolutely requires planning that is gender specific. It's also where it's both a blessing and a curse that women have the advantage of longevity.

When you went through cash flow analysis, you saw what your cost of living is right now. However, some of those expenses are going to change in retirement. In general, life in retirement costs about 80 percent of what your life costs currently.

To estimate the total amount of money needed for your retirement account, there are a couple rules of thumb for savings and withdrawals from your portfolio.

First, an industry rule of thumb for withdrawals from your portfolio is the Four Percent Rule. Withdrawing about 4 percent from your portfolio annually over a thirty-year period has been determined to be a sustainable amount, given that the portfolio is invested and returns at least inflation plus 4 percent. What this means is if, for example, you have a million dollars saved, you can take $40,000 out every year without affecting the principle. If a client needs more than $40,000 a year to live on—bearing in mind that those numbers are taxable—then they need to save more than a million dollars while they are still working.

NerdWallet and Kiplingers have very helpful online retirement calculators for walking you through how much you spend and what you have right now.

Another helpful rule of thumb is the Rule of 72, which gives an idea of how long it will take for you to save the amount you need. If you divide the return you are earning on your portfolio into 72, that tells you how many years it will take for you to double your portfolio. If your portfolio is currently earning 5 percent, divided by 72, that is 6.9 years, or 7 years. If you have $10,000 and it's making 5 percent right now, then you know that it should double in seven years.

Once you've put numbers to some of the things that are important to you, you can see how much it will likely cost to fund these things, against what you have available now. If there are significant gaps in your ability to fund any of them, you will have to choose which of your goals should get priority.

When having this conversation with clients, I often advise them that, contrary to what they've been told by other planners, retirement may not be the most important priority right now. Many of them are in the stage of life when retirement is years away. While there is a lot of pressure to max out your 401(k) contributions, remember that there is only so much money available to fund your goals as well as your regular life. If a client is twenty or thirty years away from retiring, retirement planning may take a back seat to buying a house or paying for their child's college education. We'll need to balance the funding for different goals based on priority of when these goals need to happen.

That doesn't mean that I advise the client to ignore retirement planning altogether. In fact, quite the opposite. If we make a conscious decision to prioritize a goal over retirement, we have a plan in place of how to manage savings for retirement once the priority goal is funded. Maybe right now, rather than maxing out their 401(k) at $18,500 per year, they will contribute $10,000 a year and use the remaining $8,500 to save for a house down payment, or fund a 529 for their child's education. But once that shorter term goal is met, we will ratchet up the savings for retirement. Well before decisions about how to fund a goal are made, we have thought through what steps we'll need to take and when.

No one can have everything all at once, no matter how much money they make. It's a matter of figuring out how much money you have to put toward certain goals right now and choosing on a yearly basis how much of that money should be allocated to each of them. If a client is funding that house down payment account for four years, we will want to have a plan around savings for retirement and any other goals they might have. In five years, when that goal of the house is funded, they'll go back and begin maxing out their 401(k).

In the case of my client Sophie, who wanted to quit work but couldn't afford to, the timeline for when she could make the transition to working for herself was dependent on when she had enough cash to fully fund building a new house. She figured out all the details around how much the building would cost, from purchasing the land, to the architecture, to the development. "We knew the house had to come first. It took everything, even all of my bonus money." Some planners might have said, "Well, she's certainly not positioning herself for retirement this way," but we had a priority, and it was the house first. When that goal was finished, her attention was now directed toward funding her retirement. Before any money was directed to a particular goal, we had thought through what was important to her, when each goal needed to be funded, how we were going to fund it, and what steps we would need to take to make up for lost time. We had a plan in place before we made these important financial decisions.

THE BUDGET IS IN PLACE—WHAT'S NEXT?

Once the budget is in place, you have to engage whole-heartedly with it. Whereas, before you were simply tracking your expenses and looking for trends at the end of the month, now you need to check in on this budget and make sure that you are following it. The objective is to spend money differently.

I suggest you check in every couple of days and see how you're doing, at least initially. Personally, I know that after a month goes by, I'll have long since forgotten when I went to a restaurant and how much I spent on dinner. It's easy to lose track of how much money you spent and where, without checking in frequently. Awareness is key to making empowered choices and retraining yourself to spend your money in accordance with those choices.

After adhering strictly to your budget for about two months, you'll be able to identify disconnects between the goals of your budget and the reality of your life. You may need to revise the amounts you've allocated to specific categories. For example, if you find there's absolutely no way you can lower your grocery budget to a certain amount, that's fine. Increase it, then look and see where else you can make changes. Maybe you don't need to spend as much money on shopping, dining out, or on entertainment. The overall objective is to keep your discretionary spending within a certain limit so that you can fund your bigger goals. You can rearrange the way you stay within that limit as much as you like. But to be successful, you have to be present and engaged.

STRATEGIES FOR AVOIDING BUDGET DERAILMENT

For a lot of women executives, budgeting is a big change in behavior. To be frank, it can be difficult. You can expect to wind up spending more money than you had budgeted in a given area, because that's what you've been doing for a long time. I never expect anyone to completely change their lifestyle within just two months. Remember, you're trying to change long-standing habits around money. Don't be too hard on yourself—just acknowledge when you get derailed and be more aware of it next time. If you try for several months to limit your spending in a certain area, yet you keep getting derailed, don't give up. Just try another number.

Some folks will set themselves a fairly aggressive number for a specific line item like dining out. For their first month on their budget, they'll order next to nothing when they go out. By the second month, their willpower has failed them, and they spend way more on dining out than they intended. They'll be so discouraged that they'll be inclined to give up on the budget altogether.

As their advisor, I'll encourage them to simply revisit

the number. I'll help them look at the proposed budget amount versus the amount they actually spent and come up with a more livable solution that allows them to be successful. I'll also go over the other areas of their budget and encourage them on where they made progress. It's important to take encouragement even while you're holding yourself accountable.

Some strategies for staying on track include the following requirements.

BE PRESENT

Once you begin your budget, you absolutely must check in regularly. To be clear, that doesn't mean having your bookkeeper check in for you. Staying present with your money needs to be a personal endeavor—understanding your behavior, working on your habits, adjusting your plan, and celebrating all the accomplishments along the way toward funding your goals. Remember, you've been spending money in one way for a long time—the only way to change those habits is to be accountable.

SET UP AUTO CONTRIBUTIONS

When you've earmarked money in your budget for specific goals, those should be the items that you pay first. I advise every one of my clients to set up an auto transfer to fund the goal. As soon as they get paid, it triggers an automatic payment to the accounts that fund their most important goals. Doing this ensures that you will always know your big goals are funded, and it also helps prevent your discretionary spending from being derailed.

KEEP TIME HORIZONS IN MIND

Chances are, there's probably not enough money to fund everything right now. It's okay. You're just going to have to make choices about which things are most important right now. It doesn't mean those other goals won't happen. They just won't happen all at the same time.

Let's say you want to save for buying a house in a couple of years, but you'd also like to have your four-year-old daughter go to a private university. Since your daughter is a good fourteen years away from college, it may make the most sense to put more money into an account for the house, and less (for now) into the education fund. In a couple of years, once you've bought your house, you can increase the amount you're saving for her college.

Everyone sees their goals' time horizons differently. I have one client who wants to fund college for both of her young daughters. Not long ago, we sat down to review her finances and it turned out that thanks to a bad year at her law firm, she wasn't able to make the full contribution to her retirement account this year. I suggested that in light of this, she contribute less to the girls' 529 accounts. But she said she simply wasn't willing to make that change. She understands the implication of this choice—next year, when her firm does better, that money will be going to her retirement account. That's her choice, based on what is most important to her.

The process of planning is not a steady, straight path. You have to be nimble because things change. Sometimes life takes unexpected turns that require you to make different financial choices from the ones you planned on.

It's important to not get discouraged by the need to prioritize. Some things will happen now, while other things will have to wait. It doesn't mean they're never going to happen. The point is to make incremental progress wherever you can and be consistent.

ENGAGING PERSONALLY WITH THE BUDGET PROCESS

This process is about you and your spending choices. If you're not engaged in the budgeting process, you can't change your behavior. You have to go in-depth and figure out what your spending behaviors represent in your life. You have to do the work of re-categorizing those expenses if they're not showing in the correct categories.

I had one client who sent her bookkeeper in to go over her spending with me. That does no good for her—she needed to put in the work of assessing her spending habits, herself. It doesn't help to have her bookkeeper see where her money is spent; she's not the one with the problem. Real awareness and change only happen when you personally engage in the process.

DON'T BE DISCOURAGED BY WHERE YOU ARE

When you start to automatically fund goals, seeing the progress is tremendously empowering. People may start out dreading it, but they feel so empowered when they see their progress after one good month.

There will be missteps. There will be times when stuff happens you didn't budget for or you just blow it and buy something you shouldn't have. That's okay. It's not the end of the world. It is what it is. There's another month coming, and you have the power to get yourself back on track. The key is that you move in a positive direction over time with planning. It's incredibly uplifting to see the evidence that you are finally in control of your own money.

CASH FLOW MANAGEMENT

- Knowing where you spend your money allows you to make changes, so you can fund goals that are important to you.
- Write down where you think you spend your money on a monthly basis.
- Then, track your expenses for two months.
- Determine the cost of your goals. Put a dollar amount to each goal.
- Create a budget that breaks your expenses into Fixed and Discretionary. Carve out discretionary money to fund your goals and fund them first after paying fixed expenses.
- Check in on your budget often, tweak it to work best for you.
- Determine how much you can carve from your monthly budget to start funding your goals and establish monthly auto deposits into accounts for those goals.

CHAPTER FIVE

BUSINESS AND CAREER MANAGEMENT

OVERCOMING DERAILER NUMBER THREE—STRATEGICALLY PLANNING YOUR PROFESSIONAL PATH

A woman's business or career is fundamental to attaining personal and financial well-being. However, traditional financial planning firms, and most women executives, typically do not consider how management of their business or career affects financial planning at all. That is a fundamental oversight, making it a major derailer for women executives' financial success. This chapter shows how having clear goals and a strategy around your business and career are essential to a plan for your best life—after all, your business or career is the source of the finances that enable your plan's execution. Whether you are an employer or an employee, there are strategic changes you can make to maximize the money you earn to put toward funding your goals. While the output of business and career management is maximized earnings, the underlying impetus for maximized earnings is better quality of life, which may require change in your career or business. Determining and implementing strategic changes for your career or business often requires building a team of trusted advisors in various areas—this chapter will provide an overview of the types of resources you can look to for the support you need.

BARBARA'S STORY: CREATING A PATH FOR CAREER CHANGE

For years, Barbara had been wanting a lifestyle change. Her high-powered executive role no longer felt fulfilling to her. She tried taking a similar position at a different company, shifting to a different role within her company, even moving to a new city. With each change, the result was the same. She was still working constantly and taking on more responsibility.

With every move she made, Barbara found herself making more money. But the income increase didn't improve her happiness. After working with her for ten years, discussing her passions and pursuits, Barbara finally realized what she wanted out of life, something she had never considered before. She wanted to climb *down* the corporate ladder. After years of pursuing the traditional pathway to career success, she had come to a place where she defined quality of life in terms of time, rather than money. She still wanted to work, but she wanted to be in a role that demanded less of her. She wanted to work in a field that was personally meaningful to her. She wanted to move out of the city and live somewhere with a slower pace of life. Most of all, she wanted a life that allowed her to get home at a decent hour and spend time with her family, without worrying that the phone would ring at any second.

Barbara knew that a career move like this would create a big impact on her standard of living. Fortunately, Barbara had never succumbed to "lifestyle creep"—the tendency for people who make more to spend more. Every time she found herself making more money, she had put most of it away into savings. She also kept her spending habits modest.

Over the past several years, Barbara and I have worked together to plan around each change she made in her career. Before each move was made, we knew how much she actually had to get from the job in order to keep her standard of living at the time. That planning allowed her to make the choices she made.

Now that she is planning this much more significant change, our planning is just as important. Barbara is looking at taking a lower-paying job and moving with her family to a small town in Idaho. Her cost of living there will be lower, as will her salary. But lower numbers don't mean that planning is unnecessary. We've talked in detail about the amounts she'll want to set aside for her retirement fund, her expectations around fixed and discretionary expenses, and the parameters for the lifestyle she can afford once she makes this change.

After years of conversations, consistent engagement, and deep reflection about her choices, Barbara is finally in a place where she can afford to do exactly what she wants to do for her career.

WHY BUSINESS AND CAREER MANAGEMENT IS SUCH A BIG DERAILER

There are two ways business or career management affects women executives. First, it affects your ability to fund the goals that are important to you. Second, it affects your current quality of life. It's easy to think of career management as simply moving up the ladder, always chasing the next big promotion or pay raise. Far more important than that, however, is managing your career in a way that gets you closer to your dream life.

Statistics show that professionals spend one-third of their waking hours working. That being the case, it's a pretty good idea to have a job you like or that rewards you in ways beyond just money. That's why, when I talk about career and business management with clients, I ask what is important to them in their career.

Your career is absolutely tied to your lifestyle—not just how you fund it, but how you live it. Your professional well-being is not exclusive from your financial and personal well-being. That's why, when you consider how to best manage your career, it's important to start by asking the same questions as you asked about your finances at the outset: what do you want your life to look like, and what is important to you? Once you have a picture of your ideal life in mind, you can figure out what kind of career fits into that picture and create a plan around it.

Good career management is going to be different for every person. That plan, as you might expect, is created with compensation at its core. Your paycheck is the not-so-secret weapon that enables you to live your ideal life. Your career strategy starts with a close look at what you need to fund. Once you've identified that, the questions become more about quality of life. You may love being in management and want to work your way up to CEO. On the other hand, you may want to create more flexibility in your schedule and have the option of working from home.

Perhaps you want to segue into a completely different role or industry.

When you know what's important to you in your career, it's time to confront the uncomfortable facts around how you're compensated as a woman executive. Even outside the cultural conversation around a gender-based pay gap, women generally get paid less because they work less—they are far more likely than men to take time away for raising children, caring for elderly parents, or other responsibilities related to their personal lives.[17] As a result, they typically will end up with less money than men to fund their goals.

This isn't cause for discouragement. Rather, it's an opportunity for strategic planning. Career goals are very personal, but whatever it is that is most important to you, planning will ensure that you have the resources and the tools to get you where you want to be.

HOW BUSINESS AND CAREER MANAGEMENT AFFECTS FINANCIAL PLANNING

Not long ago, I ran a number of focus groups with women attorneys. A surprising number of them said that they went into law because they expected it to give them a certain quality of life. Once they got into the industry, however,

---

17   "How to take care of aging parents and yourself." Fidelity Viewpoints, accessed September 27, 2017. https://www.fidelity.com/viewpoints/personal-finance/caring-for-aging-parents

they realized that the demanding workload didn't give them time or freedom to fully enjoy the rewards it offered. They discovered that quality of life isn't measured only in money.

This is fairly common among the women executives I work with. When we begin to explore their ideal life in the professional sphere, a number of them have told me they chose their major in college based on earning potential. They graduated, got a job, and spent thirty years in an industry simply because it's what they know. For them, having a job or business they love is not so important to their overall quality of life. Instead, they value their career as a source for funding their passions and pursuits in other areas of life. Their dissatisfaction comes not from the job itself but from feeling like it leaves them no time to enjoy the quality of life that it was supposed to bring them.

Most planners never help clients make this discovery. Traditional financial planning does not spend time on the source of your income or tying your career to quality of life. The idea is that you keep doing what you're doing while your income goes to work for you, and once you've reached retirement age, you can cash in. This is a fundamental disconnect in the financial journey.

I want more for my clients than that. I help them maximize their income but not at the expense of their quality of life. That's why I help them take a close look at the opportunities within their career and get the resources they need to be successful in that career or business. However they choose to define success, they need to make strategic moves that will help them fund their goals today while gathering the tools they need to succeed in the way they define success.

DEFINING YOUR BUSINESS AND CAREER GOALS

Career management begins in the same place where we started: with passions and pursuits. Career well-being is not just about landing your ideal job. It's all the pieces—compensation, benefits, flexibility, location. If you could change your job to look exactly the way you want, what would that be? Don't be afraid to think big.

Next, consider where you are right now. What do you find satisfying about your career, and where does it not measure up to your vision? Once you understand the gaps between where you are and where you want to be, you'll be able to identify the resources you can employ to close those gaps.

Then, you'll dive into the details just as you would with any other goal. Compare where you are to what you want your job to look like three, five, and ten years from now. Consider whether or not you're being paid what you're worth, if you're working in the role you deserve, and what opportunities there are for you to maximize your earnings.

Asking these questions will help you determine the next steps. In creating a plan around career management, it's important to be aware of how career issues tend to be more complex for women and understanding how to navigate them.

As women, we face a common set of career derailers. Often, women executives don't realize that they are not paid what they deserve. I've also seen many cases where women are passed over for well-earned leadership roles in favor of men. Women tend not to negotiate for themselves well and routinely leave money on the table.

Maybe you are aware that you're facing these derailers, but you don't know what you can do about it. Rest assured that while the path to your ideal career might be complicated, it is ultimately all within your control. It's simply a matter of getting very specific and granular about your goals, understanding how those goals tie in with your personal goals, knowing the resources you need, and obtaining the skills you need to change your circumstances. Its having a plan around your career or business. As in Barbara's case, this process is likely to take years, rather than weeks. But through the process of making these intentional changes, you reap the daily benefits of knowing that you are moving toward building a career on your own terms.

I once conducted a focus group with women executives

in science, technology, engineering and math careers, commonly known as STEM. Through this focus group, I learned that most of the C-suite women in STEM had been attracted to their jobs because of their passion for the field. It was far less about making a great income, and much more about the interest and meaning they found in their work. However, their passion for their industry caused them to overlook an important issue: these women executives didn't realize they weren't getting paid as well as the men in their field. When I shared with them some amazing statistics from some studies, they were horrified. They had no idea how little they were being compensated, relative to their male peers.

Another issue is the leadership hierarchy. Compensation is typically better for those who have a higher role. But because women are often passed over for leadership roles, despite having the skills and expertise, they don't get the compensation benefits of these higher-level positions.

Again, the legal industry provides a perfect example of this. Law firms are driven by male leadership.[18] According to a 2017 study by McKinsey, 19 percent of equity partners in law firms are female, and women equity partners earn 80

---

18   Marc Brodherson, Laura McGee, Mariana Pires dos Reis, "Women in law firms." McKinsey & Company, accessed October 2017. https://www.mckinsey.com/~/media/mckinsey/global%20themes/gender%20equality/women%20in%20law%20firms/women-in-law-firms-final-103017.ashx

percent of male equity partners![19] Almost half of female attorneys call prioritizing work-life balance one of the greatest challenges to their professional success. The number of women partners has stagnated for a number of years. This affects not only the current leadership staff; it also has an impact on future leaders within the firm. In addition, fewer women partners means fewer mentors or sponsors for future women attorneys.

The same patterns hold true in STEM. In these industries, women tend to gravitate to more managerial, less technical positions—not because they aren't interested in the technical side, but because they lack mentors or sponsors to pull them up to those positions. However, much of the money and power in STEM is on the technical side. As a result, you have the situation all too common amongst major STEM corporations where the board of directors has no women on it. It's almost as if they have a "no women on our board" rule.[20] *Fortune* magazine reports that a full 60 percent of US "unicorn" companies have no women on their boards.[21]

---

19   https://www.americanbar.org/content/dam/aba/marketing/women/current_glance_statistics_january2017.authcheckdam.pdf

20   *Understanding Society: Innovation Panel, Waves 1-8, 2008-2015. 7th Edition.* University of Essex. Institute for Social and Economic Research (2016) UK Data Service. SN: 6849, https://www.understandingsociety.ac.uk/documentation/citation

21   Erica Swallow, "The most exclusive boys' club: America's largest startups." *Fortune.* accessed March 16, 2015. http://fortune.com/2015/03/16/unicorns-women-boards/

Reflecting on these challenges is not meant to make you despair. Personally, I make it a rule not to play the victim card. Rather than complain about how unfair the situation is, I advise clients to look at it squarely so that they can get the tools to deal with it. Once you know what the obstacles in your industry are, you can create a plan to tackle them incrementally.

HOW BUSINESS AND CAREER GOALS INTERACT WITH OTHER DERAILERS AND SOLUTIONS

Your career goals and the challenges presented in your industry are factors that will come into play as you're trying to improve your quality of life as a whole. Career is an important part of our quality of life, and it interacts with the other major derailers in determining your overall quality of life. Your career success can affect the prioritization and the time horizons of every goal you listed within your passions and pursuits—the personal goals as well as the professional ones.

Cash flow management plays a major role in career management. Your ability to make smart decisions with money dictates the choices you have in your career. After all, it's hard to make bold career moves if you're afraid of jeopardizing your ability to pay your bills. But when your spending is under control, and you've built up a good emergency fund, you feel much more empowered to ask for the promotion, move across the country, or make the transition to a new industry. In the case of Barbara, having her lifestyle expenses under control allowed her to take a lower paying job that provides the overall quality of life she desires.

I have a client who spent many years as a lawyer at a large law firm before choosing to take a less demanding job as an attorney with her state government, making about one-third of what she was making before. She's not a big spender, and she had saved a little slush fund that would carry her through the period of time when she was adjusting to her new cash flow. She had to plan for this move, but in exchange for giving up a lot of income, she obtained a quality of life that she absolutely loves. Having extra money saved in her emergency fund helped her ease into this new career.

As with everything else, there's give and take. This client's decision meant she couldn't afford to contribute a dime to her retirement account. It's been five years since she took the new role, and she is now able to fully max out her 401(k)—for a time, though, it was something that had to be put aside. We didn't have the money, but we ultimately knew she'd get to the point where she could afford to do it. This is exactly what is meant by making choices.

STRATEGIC MANAGEMENT OF TAXES

Strategic management of your taxes and investments, whether as an employer or an employee, can maximize and grow the money you have available to fund your goals.

It goes without saying that tax strategy begins with minimizing how much you pay. There are some very intuitive ways to accomplish this—contributing to retirement accounts, for example, not only saves for your future but also lowers your taxable income. The benefits that come with your choice of career will affect your strategy around taxes. Your employer may offer you tax benefits like health savings accounts, flex spending accounts, or dependent care allowance. They may have a 401(k), a profit-sharing plan, or a cash balance plan. Whatever it is, there will be certain tax opportunities for you to maximize. You want to take those opportunities to lower your taxable income.

If, like most women executives, you have the majority of your assets in your 401(k) or retirement plan, you need to make sure you have a good strategy around how much you're putting into that fund. You also need a good strategy around how you're investing that money. The federal government dictates how much you can contribute to all these various accounts, based on your age. This year, for example, anyone under the age of fifty can contribute up to $18,500 to a 401(k) on a qualified retirement plan.

There are different retirement plans with certain maximum amounts. If you are more senior in a company, you may have access to more benefits, such as a profit-sharing plan or deferred compensation plans. There are employee stock plans where you can buy stock for a reduced price. Whatever other benefits your employer may provide, you need a strategy deciding if you should participate in them, and if so, how much. The unique financial benefits of your career are not a one-size-fits-all, just as your ideal career is not a one-size-fits-all. You need a whole strategy around what's best for you, given what you have to work with now and the goals you have for your future.

BUSINESS AND CAREER MANAGEMENT STRATEGIES

When you begin to look at career management strategies, the first step is to begin considering your job as a compensation source. Your job is the tool that generates all your money. So, your first order of business is to maximize what that job is creating for you. Keep in mind that compensation comes in many forms. This may include flexible work schedules, benefits, etc. You want to be managing your entire career or business so it suits you and your life best.

The next thing to do is create a clear plan that will get you to the next role that you want. You may need to strategize for more senior roles; you may even want to contemplate a career change if it means better alignment with your overall goals.

You also have to consider how your ultimate career goal will affect the big picture of your quality of life. There has to be a balance between your ideal career and the goals that are most important to you. All planning is ultimately about choices and weighing the work you want to do against the lifestyle that will make you the happiest.

Personally, I could have stayed at my former company a lot longer, if money had been the only consideration. I was making good money there, but my quality of life suffered. I made a conscious decision to launch my own company so that I could do things on my own terms. It was a trade-off, but for me, there was no comparison. However, I also didn't just head off into the sunset as soon as I'd made my choice. I planned out my transition in a way that allowed me to maintain my lifestyle and fulfill my responsibilities while pursuing my ideal life.

A wellness expert from Kaiser Permanente spoke at my women's group not long ago and talked about how our anxiety flows right through us to those we love. If you find yourself unhappy in your current work situation, it's important to know that it's not just you who might be miserable—your kids pick up on your misery, as well, and it can be quite harmful for them. This is just one reason why it doesn't serve any purpose to grind out your working life in a position that you hate. When you're dreading getting up in the morning, when you look at your job and think, "What else can I do? This is all I know," it has long-term repercussions on more lives than just your own. The first-wave (e.g., first year) findings of a study on this topic have just been published. One of the data points the study reported was that the happiness of children in a household (aged ten to twenty-one, living at home) is significantly affected by the happiness of their mother, or at least her happiness in terms of her marriage.[22]

Despite the fact that many women are not fulfilled in their careers, it's not often that they actually talk about it. It's like money, which people don't talk about either. This is where community can become so valuable. Many years ago, I had a bad day that made me want to quit on the spot. My peer group of women was meeting for dinner that night, but I just wanted to go home. However, I made myself drive to the restaurant, and to my own surprise, shared the situation with the women there. They offered not only sympathy, but some truly constructive advice based on their own experiences. It showed me yet again the importance of sharing things that make us feel vulnerable. You're far from alone—in fact, the things you experience are probably more common than you know.

---

22   https://www.understandingsociety.ac.uk/

It is possible to have a fulfilling career, both now and in the future, that offers the quality of life you value. Building this career starts with asking what you want out of your job, and it continues with examining the details of how that job will allow you to live life on your terms. You may need more money for your current role, you may want a more senior role, or you may just be in a career that is completely wrong for you. Think about the overall quality of life you want and let that drive where you wind up professionally.

Career change management is motivated by desire to have a better quality of life and be happier, but it also has to include the compensation piece. I'm not saying just get out there and do whatever you love at the expense of being able to pay your bills. I believe there's a balance. Money should be part of your decision, but it certainly should not be the only driver. As businesswomen, our jobs affect so many different aspects of our experience, from compensation to quality of life. That's why it's so important to sit down and think about what's really important to you. Equally important is knowing that if you feel as though you're not working where you want to be, you're absolutely not alone in that experience.

After my focus group with women attorneys, at least one woman actually left the industry and went into a completely unrelated field that she absolutely loves. She had been in law a long time and had been very successful, but the reflection we did during that focus group provoked her to make a life-changing decision. She lives in a beautiful home in a beach community, and she started renting it out to vacationers. She also knew a lot of people who were interested in renting out their high-end homes, and she started helping these people make their homes available for short-term rentals. (This, by the way, was before Airbnb started—she effectively anticipated a whole new industry.) By following something she loved, she went into a whole new career, one that she found so much more fulfilling, and she is able to afford the quality of life important to her.

Considering career change is just another phase in the big picture of financial planning. However, if you can't figure out what's not satisfying about your career, you're not stuck.

Among the many great resources I work with, there is a woman who helps people identify what their passions are, and then she finds a career that fits those passions. If you're not happy where you are but don't know what you want to do instead, she leads you through a series of exercises on how to find fulfillment.

I brought her in to speak to my women's group once.

Despite our group's diversity—attorneys, scientists, engineers, a real cross-section of industries—she was able to walk us through the exercises she has created to help people determine what their passion is, and whether they are living true to that passion in their current career.

She asked a question that many women executives have an incredibly hard time answering: "What do you do for fun?" It seems so basic, but when all you do is work and take care of other people, you may find, like many of the women in our group that day, that you can't answer it. Amid all the things that are important to you, there still has to be a "you" in the equation.

If you know you're not happy in your job but can't put your finger on what makes you unhappy, you've encountered a crucial opportunity to step back and assess. "What makes me happy?" may seem like a frivolous question, but it's actually incredibly important. You only have one life, and you are fortunate in having the opportunity to make choices.

HAVE A PLAN

Over the past several years, there has been a lot of hype about following your passion, followed by a lot of skepticism about whether that approach to life makes sense. If you're like most women executives, you're skeptical of the idea that you can just walk out your office door tomorrow and begin doing whatever you've been dreaming about. While you may feel more passion about your profession, you'll be sacrificing quality of life in other ways. You need to sit down and think through what you want to do, what skills and tools you need to be able to do it, where the opportunities are for you to do it, and how to build the steps between where you are now and where you want to be.

No matter how long you've been in your career, you're never stuck. If career change is what makes sense for you to live a fulfilling life, it's entirely possible to make that change through strategic planning and incremental change.

Remember Brenda, my client who wanted to be a career coach? Despite knowing exactly what she wants to do, she can't simply walk out the door and start her new practice. Doing so would mean a tremendous cost to her quality of life, not to mention her ability to provide for herself and her family. That's why we've created a plan for her to get the skills she needs over time, while incrementally beginning to take on clients, without giving up her current job until she's confident that her new business can bring the income she needs. She's also saving money, living a little below her means so that she can put aside funds that will get her through the early start-up phase of her new coaching practice.

RECONFIGURE OTHER GOALS

Strategic planning around career is not only important for your present happiness. It also helps you stay on track with other goals. One obvious thing to consider is retirement—when you're well into one career, changing into a new one will almost certainly have an impact on when you can retire. You need to have a plan in place around how you will continue saving for retirement, one that takes into account your prospective age and health.

SEGUEING INTO A NEW ROLE

When looking at career strategy, it's important to look at all aspects of your current situation to assess what your best move might be. For you, happiness might not require something as dramatic as leaving your industry and starting a completely new business. It might be as simple as taking a different role within your current company, one that is more aligned with what you want, without giving up the paycheck or the benefits that you have accrued.

This is another reason why incremental change is so valuable. It allows you to make a transition gradually, to test out your potential happiness before you make a huge, life-altering decision. It's important to go into career possibilities with open eyes—you never know what might happen or what you might realize. It might even be as simple as taking on a side project within your current company or doing some consulting on the side. If those options don't work for you, there's nothing to say you can't decide that you're happy where you are. The most important thing is to create a career on your own terms. Knowing that you are in charge of your professional trajectory makes the biggest difference in your day-to-day happiness at work.

ADOPT A NEW RETIREMENT STRATEGY

When it comes to leveraging your career, retirement is a key consideration. However, that consideration doesn't necessarily mean retiring as early as you possibly can. Most of my clients don't plan on retiring. In fact, 53 percent of women plan to retire after age sixty-five or not at all. They want to be able to choose how much they work, but they don't want to just stop working when they reach a certain age.

This "at will" retirement approach is becoming far more common. Seventy-two percent of baby boomer pre-retirees say that they want to keep working after they retire. Rather than work themselves to death and retire as early as possible, they prefer to work on their own terms and have a better quality of life right now.

My own dad is a great example of this. He's eighty years old and still runs a business. He tried to retire (by cutting his schedule down to just three days a week), and he was not happy with it. He loves working and doesn't want to stop. Honestly, I think that's what keeps him so mentally sharp. Studies have found significant anti-aging benefits to continuing working as we age.

Most executive women have worked hard to get to where they are, fueled by skill, expertise, and a desire to help people. Work gives them a tremendous sense of satisfaction and purpose. It isn't something they want to give up altogether—they simply want to be able to call the shots on when, where, and how often they work.

At the same time, it would be irresponsible not to recognize that there will be a time for all of us at which you can't work at the pace you do today. As you age, working fifty or sixty hours per week will not be an option for you. It's important to acknowledge that reality, to understand how that future should affect your retirement and savings today.

As always, your unique definition of quality of life presents many unique opportunities and challenges from a financial planning perspective. If you can count on continuous income over a longer period of time, you might be able to spend more now. If you want to make a major shift in your career, it might make more sense to prioritize shorter-term savings over retirement savings.

No matter what you want your career to look like—getting paid more for your current role, segueing to a different role, getting promoted, or building your own company—that goal changes how you need to plan for your retirement.

RESOURCES TO HELP CHANGE OR MANAGE YOUR CAREER

There are many people who can help you change or strategically manage your career depending on your goals. A team of trusted advisors is indispensable and can include the following people.

CERTIFIED FINANCIAL PLANNER™

You need to leverage your career to live the quality of life you want. A CERTIFIED FINANCIAL PLANNER™ (CFP®) professional will help you with the resources you need to leverage your career and make sure the financial framework of your life collaborates with your quality of life as a whole. The CFP® professional can help you find awareness around what you want your business or career to look like, help you figure out what your goals are, and work around that to create the life you want, both now and down the road. This will involve strategy around the compensation or revenue piece, managing the benefits offered, minimizing taxes, and having an incremental plan that leverages your business or career, so you can live your ideal life.

EXECUTIVE PLACEMENT FIRM

If your professional interest lies in moving up the food chain to more senior roles or to another company, you need the services of an executive placement firm. A lot of women overlook this resource, perhaps because they don't have as much input from mentors and sponsors to tell them about the value of such firms as a career-shaping tool.

This doesn't just apply to C-suite roles. Regardless of your industry, if you're middle management or above, you need to make use of this resource to strategize successfully around your career.

Another common mistake is to wait on contacting an executive placement firm until you're sick of your job and ready to move on. In the words of a woman I know who owns a highly regarded executive placement firm for STEM executives, "I can't help you if you say you want to leave your role now. I don't know who you are, and I don't necessarily have a job available." Executive placement folks are not the same as "head hunters"—they work for corporations, not for you. When a corporation needs a new staff member, they look to these firms for recommendations of candidates that are already known to them.

That's why it's crucial to reach out to an executive placement firm long before you ever want to make a transition. You don't get the C-suite role by just sending your resume and hoping that somebody will find you—it's all done through cultivating relationships. Identify the top placement people in your field, meet with them for coffee, and get an updated resume in their hands to make sure they know you and your strengths. It doesn't hurt to keep in touch with them periodically, as well. When companies reach out to the firm looking for candidates to fill their top roles, they'll know when you're the best person to place.

COACHES

Once you've identified where you want to go with your career or business, a coach will help you fill in the gaps, whether that means obtaining technical training, cultivating leadership potential, managing and implementing your business plan, or maybe simply helping you build confidence.

There are two types of coaches that will help you develop different aspects of career strategy. One type gets into the nuts and bolts of a company and examines it for challenges and opportunities, while the other gets to know an individual personally with an eye to getting them where they want to be in their life and career. A business coach offers guidance regarding how best to run your company—how best to generate revenue, what business growth should look like, and how to retool your current business model for better success. A career or lifestyle coach guides you in building a specific skillset that helps you obtain the roles you want, such as technical expertise or negotiation, or helping you identify what industry or role you might find fulfilling.

I'm a huge proponent of using a coach as a resource—at this point, most of my clients retain a coach to develop the skills they need to advance their career. Whatever you might have identified as challenges in your profession, coaches can give you the tools for overcoming those challenges and getting to a place where you can work on your own terms.

MENTORS AND SPONSORS

In today's world, women executives don't get to the leadership roles they want simply by being available and willing. They need someone who advocates for them, who brings up their name, sings their praises, and speaks to their qualifications. They need a sponsor.

A sponsor is someone whom you can count on to put you in the right meeting, make the right introductions for you, and make sure you're receiving the visibility, awareness, and recognition you deserve.

It's a sad but true fact that for most women in the work-place, recognition won't happen on its own. In addition, women executives have to be much more intentional about finding a sponsor. Because most leadership positions are held by men, more sponsor relationships naturally come about for men. As a result, you wind up with more men in leadership roles, and the cycle continues.

It would be great if there were more women leaders who could naturally form sponsor relationships with other women. However, that won't happen until women exec-utives take initiative in finding male sponsors to advocate for them in obtaining those leadership roles.

While a sponsor is someone who speaks on your behalf, a mentor is someone who offers you training and insight on how to build your career—much like a coach, but from an insider perspective.

While mentorship is undoubtedly valuable for women executives, sponsors can be much harder to find. Women are great at finding ways to improve their skills, but they also need advocates that help them use those skills in the right positions. Regardless, both mentors and sponsors are key ways to get where you want to be in business.

In order to secure either mentors or sponsors, you have to know where to look. For mentor relationships, I suggest that women in specific industries join industry organizations, which frequently offer mentorship programs. They may set you up one-on-one with a potential mentor, or they may invite you to a group meeting where you can form relationships on your own.

Sponsorships can be harder to come by. These are usually people who work within your own organization or company, though they could also be a peer in your networking group. The important thing is that your sponsor be someone whose opinion will hold weight with your organization's leadership, who can be counted on to vouch for your qualifications to your company or client base.

ACCOUNTANT

Career strategy involves making the most efficient use of your income during each phase of moving toward the career you want. Certified Public Accountants (CPAs) are absolutely critical in this process, helping you minimize taxes and maximize income.

This is particularly true if you run your own company or firm. A CPA will be able to tell you how much you should be paying yourself, based on the taxes you want to pay. This is not something an individual can do alone—the tax code is simply too complex and changes too often to navigate on your own.

However, a CPA is still a crucial resource for those who are W2 or 1099 employees. No working woman executive can create a sound career strategy without advice on how to maximize deductions. The amount you can save in deductions plays a huge role in determining the income you need to earn in order to create the quality of life you want.

I brought a CPA in for a new client a couple years ago to work with me in creating an array of different retirement plan options for her firm. My goal was to maximize how much my client could save for the things she wanted to fund; his goal was to determine how much she should pay herself, based on how much she would be taxed on that number after contributing to her defined benefit plan and her retirement plan.

ATTORNEYS

A business attorney knows something very important that you likely don't know: how best to structure your company. While I work with some of the most accomplished women executives in industry today, few of them are what I would call "born businesswomen." While they are top in their specific fields, they are far less skilled in running a company.

A business lawyer will know how to help you with everything from big-picture issues, such as managing risk, to minutiae such as filing the paperwork required for corporations every year.

NETWORKING

Networking is critical for several reasons. It expands your business opportunities. It allows you to meet role models, mentors, or sponsors. It puts you in the company of other business leaders to make social connections, exchange resources, and provide like-minded support.

I once heard from an executive placement professional that executives should be networking every single night. Clearly, that's not an option for most people, particularly for women executives who have families and a personal life. However, this advice underscored the point that women executives have to do more than collect a drawer full of business cards. Networking is about the quality of your connections, not the quantity. Meaningful, ongoing personal connections with like-minded professionals are an important tool in building the career you want.

Meaningful networking will look different for every woman executive. Personally, I have a very small group of trusted resources within my network whom I stay in touch with by going to lunch, reaching out for advice, and generally staying in front of them. The main thing is to stay current and connected with the people who can help you accomplish what you want in your career.

WHEN YOU KNOW WHAT YOU WANT, CHANGE IS POSSIBLE

Career strategy sounds like a big task to tackle. In reality, though, it is an incremental process like any other aspect of financial planning. It starts with knowing what you want your career or business to look like. Invest some time in figuring out what kind of work is fulfilling to you and what situation would be ideal for the quality of life you want.

Next, take a close look at where you are right now. This is how you will see where the gaps lie between where you currently are and where you want to be. Don't be afraid of confronting those gaps. Instead, spend time detailing how you can create bridges that allow you to move forward, one step at a time.

Ask what your challenges are in getting what you want out of your career. If you're not getting paid enough, identify the skills you need to negotiate a raise or obtain a promotion to a higher-paying role. If there are gender-specific challenges in your industry (and there almost certainly are), identify them and get the tools you need to overcome them.

Once you've identified your challenges, get to work finding

the right resources who can provide counsel, assistance, and insight in overcoming each challenge. If you want to change your job, find someone who can help you identify the right role for you. If you need business development skills, find a coach who specializes in training and counsel around those skills. If you aren't sure that your business is structured in the best way for maximizing earning potential, engage a business attorney and a CPA.

Finally, seek out a network that can provide you with the moral support you need to stay motivated. I particularly advise becoming a member of a community of like-minded women executives. Consider thoughtfully where might be the best place for you to spend time on a regular basis to get the kind of support you need, whether that be social connection, help with business opportunities, or anything else.

Lastly, put your plan together. This is critical because it will drive your quality of life as well as the compensation that will pay for it.

Know that if you're not happy where you are, you're far from alone in feeling that way. Allow yourself to think about what you would like and just incrementally make changes. As long as you know what it is you want, you can start to make change in the right direction.

In this country, we are incredibly lucky—we have the ability to do just about anything we want. If you don't have the skillset, you can get it. If you don't know the right people, you can find a way to meet them. It's all up to you to decide what's important to you, determine what you need to obtain it, and make the choices that lead you to it, one step at a time.

Figuring out how to manage your career is important—it's what's going to allow you to live the life you want.

BUSINESS AND CAREER MANAGEMENT
STRATEGICALLY MANAGE AND LEVERAGE YOUR GREATEST FINANCIAL TOOL TO ALIGN WITH YOUR GOALS AND FUND YOUR IDEAL LIFE.

- Determine what you want your career or business to be.
- Assess where you are now professionally.
- Identify gaps you see: these may include industry specific challenges, compensation pieces, gender issues, lack of specific skills.
- Get the professional resources you need based on the gaps you identify.
- Become a member of a community of like-minded women.
- Put together a plan of action.

CHAPTER SIX

TAX STRATEGIES AND INVESTMENT MANAGEMENT

When you have leveraged your income as best you can through compensation and lifestyle, there still remains the question of where it goes once you've earned it. Tax strategy is all about minimizing the amount you give away, while investment management is about efficiently deploying your money to work for you.

Tax strategies and investment management are typically not fundamental areas of derailment for women executives, but they are integral considerations and key tools that should be leveraged to attain your goals. Ultimately, tax strategies and investment decisions must be derivative of and answer to the goals of your plan, and they must interact closely with your cash flow management and business/career management.

Not long ago, I met a woman who said she'd love for me to create a financial plan for her, since she had no idea if she was financially secure or on track for retirement. However, she didn't feel ready to leave her current financial advisor, a stockbroker with whom she'd worked for thirty years.

As we talked, it became clear to me that her current advisor doesn't understand her goals—he invests money without tying it to any financial planning for her. When I asked her about this, she said that her goals had never come up during their consultations.

It's unfortunate, but this woman's financial advisor is absolutely typical of financial advisors from the brokerage house side of my industry. The traditional focus tends to be on investing, without digging deeper to identify and plan for the many goals clients have.

Frankly, I find this to be a major disservice, especially when it comes to hardworking women executives who are counting on their planner to help them maximize the money they earn. If you're like many women executives, you may be blowing through money every month without even knowing it, thanks to overpaying taxes and investment choices that aren't right for you.

No financial planner, no matter how knowledgeable or experienced, can offer effective solutions without first understanding the unique goals you have for the life you want to live. Tax and investment strategies are absolutely tied to your overall goals—the decisions around these pieces are based on what you're trying to accomplish in building the life you want to live.

FINANCIAL PLANNER, FINANCIAL ADVISOR, BROKER...WHAT'S THE DIFFERENCE?

Do you know the difference between these roles? In a nutshell, they are differentiated by their responsibility to a client.

- Brokers and insurance agents can and do sell financial products, for which they receive a commission. They are not required to put the client's interests before their own. They can recommend investments with higher fees, riskier features, and lower returns if they get a higher commission, even if those investments are not the best choice for a client.

- Financial advisors and financial planners can vary broadly. They can have professional designations, or not; sell products, or not; provide financial planning, or just manage investments; charge fee-only, or charge combination of fee and commission. One thing to consider when determining if a financial planner or advisor has your best interest at heart is if their firm is a Registered Investment Advisor, which means they are required by law to put clients' interests first. This is what is called a fiduciary, and it means they are required to put your needs before theirs. You can ensure that your advisor or potential advisor is a fiduciary by asking to see their ADV (a form filed with the SEC).

This chapter is all about choosing your investments and minimizing your tax burden based on the unique goals you have for the life you want to live. That said, this chapter is in no way meant to provide tax advice, nor should you expect to understand everything about tax and investment strategies after reading this chapter. It's an incredibly dense topic that requires an expert to manage.

Rather, this chapter is intended to show the importance of having a strategy around these pieces. Instead, I strongly recommend taking the principles in this section into a discussion with your accountant and financial planner.

I look at each client's life as a puzzle with many pieces—every element works together to create quality of life as they define it. Your taxes and investments are essentially a puzzle within that bigger puzzle—each tax strategy and investment account should be considered within a client's overall strategy.

This chapter will offer some considerations for better managing your taxes and investments. These considerations will tie in with the solutions we've already discussed in Chapters 3-5 about overcoming the four major derailers. Bear in mind, however, that this chapter shouldn't be seen as tax or investment advice as such. Rather, it's meant to be an overview of tax and investment management concepts that are worth considering within your overall financial plan. Tax strategy and investment strategy are very personal and are based on each individual's situation and goals. I strongly recommend you speak with your accountant and your financial planner to determine the best strategy for you.

TAX STRATEGIES

According to the old adage, it's not what you make, it's what you keep. We talked about this in Chapter 3 regarding cash flow, keeping spending meaningful and allocating money to what's important to you. When it comes to taxes, keeping more of what you make comes down to two major strategies: lowering your taxable income and deferring taxes on gains.

FIRST THINGS FIRST: FIND A GREAT CPA

In my opinion, no one should be doing their own taxes. Tax law is incredibly complex, and it changes frequently. In order to take full advantage of the opportunities available to you, it's essential to find a good CPA who can work in tandem with your planner not only to minimize your tax liability but also choose the most tax-efficient investments.

In the Appendix, you'll find a list of questions that are beneficial to ask when interviewing potential CPAs.

Employer-Provided Benefits

Seventy-five percent of women have a tax-advantaged retirement plan available through their employer but only contribute a small amount of their salary to it. In fact, a tax-advantaged retirement plan is just one of many potential employer-provided benefits you may have access to. To make sure you're taking full advantage of these prime opportunities to keep more of the money that you make, consider the following:

- Know what benefits your employer provides so you can take advantage of them. These may include retirement plans, health savings accounts, flexible spending accounts, deferred compensation, child care credits, ESPP plans, stock options, and others. You can find out what benefits are available to you by reaching out to your company's human resources department.
- Leverage your financial planner and CPA to help determine how you can maximize the benefits you're given. Knowing the contribution limits in each employer-provided plan, and how they fit into your cash flow and tax situation, will let you take best advantage of the benefits available to you.
- If you are your own employer, your financial planner and CPA can collaborate to help you create options for your firm.

Tax-Efficient Investments

Not all investments are created equal. It's important when choosing investments to look not only at how much you can gain over a period of time but at how your investment and gains will be taxed. The following are a few things to consider:

- Some investments provide tax-free income, while other investments are tax-efficient by the nature of how they are structured.
- How long you hold an investment can change the rate at which your gains are taxed.
- Talk to your CPA about how offsetting gains and losses in investments can lower your taxes.

Tax-Efficient Accounts

If you have both retirement and taxable accounts (nonretirement), you can choose to "locate" your investments in the most tax efficient account, which may lead to tax savings and increased investment returns.

- Talk to your planner about which types of investments should go into which types of accounts.
- Different accounts also have different tax implications when you want to take money out. Your CPA and financial planner can help you choose the best account depending on the goal of the money in the account.

Maximize Tax Deductions

You may have heard that deductions have been greatly impacted by the recent changes in tax law. The requirements around deductions have become even more complex, making it imperative to work with an expert so that you don't miss opportunities for tax savings.

One very important item to discuss with your CPA is whether itemized deductions will matter to you, given the change to the standard deduction.

Your tax filing status can make a significant difference in how much tax you are required to pay. Moreover, as life changes, your filing status may also need to change. Your CPA will be able to advise you in the following ways:

- Ensuring your business entity structure is the most tax-efficient for you.
- Making sure your personal filing status is the most tax-efficient for you.
- Navigating life transitions (such as marriage, divorce, widowhood, or gaining a dependent) to ensure that you take advantage of the filing status that offers the most benefits to your new situation.
- Making sure that your tax liability reflects any unconventional circumstances in your life, such as assuming responsibility for the care of aging parents or adult children.

- Timing your charitable deductions so that they can offer you the greatest tax benefit.

Apply Expenses and Losses Strategically

Many women executives don't realize that expenses impact more than just your bottom line. How you apply business expenses can lower your taxable income, which means keeping more of the money that you make. With your CPA's help, you can strategically apply expenses, as well as incremental investment losses, in the following ways:

- Maximize business expenses to lower your qualified business income.
- Determine whether you're financially better off taking an investment loss now or carrying it forward.

BUSINESS AND CAREER COMPENSATION

It's important to consider tax strategy around your job's compensation options. Many benefits are taxed differently, making this another area where an experienced CPA will prove their value. Here are just a few of the issues where you'll want expert advice:

- Having a strategy around ESPP, RSUs, and stock options that will maximize income and minimize taxes.

- Deciding whether to participate in these benefits.
- Planning in advance for how deferred compensation options may be taxed, depending on how they are paid out.

INVESTMENT MANAGEMENT

The goal behind investing is simple: you want your money to grow over time. It makes sense that you should allocate your money to a place that is primarily growth, while still keeping a safety blanket in place.

At the same time, your investment choices should be based on your personal goals, your risk tolerance, and your time horizon. This means that every investor's plan will be different.

I have a client who is forty, quite young in terms of retirement timing. She has the opportunity to be a little more aggressive with her investments that are earmarked for funding her retirement than, for example, someone who is planning to retire in just five or ten years. However, this client is absolutely risk averse. Accordingly, we chose to invest her portfolio for retirement more in keeping with somebody who is fifteen years older than she is. That's what she's comfortable with—to put it in terms we're familiar with by now, those conservative investments contribute to her overall quality of life. This may mean she needs to work longer if we don't get the growth in her portfolio that will allow her to stop working at a certain time. For her, this is a trade-off she is willing to make.

Experience has shown me that many women are risk-averse when it comes to investing. This poses a challenge to funding retirement and other long-term goals. Between the average woman's longevity and the unique financial challenges she is likely to face, a concentrated portfolio of low-risk assets like cash simply won't grow fast enough. This is where financial education can be a tremendous help. Having the guidance of a financial planner will instill the confidence you need for your future.

Another of my clients wants to buy a house in two years, a very short-time horizon. She has some money saved up and is now saving more for a down payment. Every month, she saves more money, and it sits in an investment account. Some of the money is invested for another goal, but a big chunk of it sits in cash and earns next to nothing. For her purposes, that situation is perfect—she doesn't have the ability to lose that money and make it back in two years.

Ultimately, your goals should dictate how your money is invested. Here are a few things to consider when talking with your CERTIFIED FINANCIAL PLANNER™ professional about investment strategies:

- Determine how much you need for your goal, when you need the money, and your appetite for risk.
- Decide on an investment philosophy to help you create an overall asset allocation.
- Decide on your asset allocation. This is your mix of stocks, bonds, cash, and real estate based on your goal. This is based on your goals/risk tolerance/and when you need the money.
- Determine what type of accounts you have for your goals (retirement, taxable, cash) and invest the most tax-efficient way in each, plus locate the investments in the most tax-efficient account.
- Revisit your portfolio annually to make sure it has stayed on track and make any changes needed to bring it back in line.

Make Your Income Sources Work Together

I look at investment strategy as a holistic strategy—no single goal works without regard for the other goals a client has in mind. Whatever your goals might include—funding your child's college, buying a house or a new car, or retiring—you will have accounts earmarked for each one. However, accounts don't work in a vacuum. Even though you might invest money specifically for a house down payment in one account and have different investments based on your retirement goals in another, they all need to be considered together.

There are different investments you can use to fund your goals, including stocks, bonds, cash, and real estate. Each one has a different purpose based on differing levels of liquidity and volatility. As you figure out what you're comfortable with around all of these pieces, you can create your own investment philosophy—the set of goals and ideals that guide the who, what, where, when, and why of your investing.

For instance, you may decide that you only want to invest in companies that are socially responsible. If reading about the market gyrations makes you sick to your stomach, you may want to steer clear of high-risk investments. Spend some time here with your CFP ® professional and CPA to determine what is important to you before investing.

Personally, I don't believe in stock picking. Instead, I use low-cost, high-quality, time-tested liquid investments, such as passively managed mutual funds, ETFs, and index funds. Low cost, tax-efficient, liquid investments like these help you get to where you want to be much sooner.

There's a story I love sharing with clients that helps illustrate my philosophy. In 2007, Warren Buffet made a $1 million wager with the head of a hedge fund company called Protégé Partners.[23] Buffet bet that over a ten-year period, a passively managed index fund would outperform a selection of hedge funds. Buffet's chosen investment returned 7.1 percent annually over the period, versus 2.1 percent by Protégé Partners. The combination of low cost and passive management outperformed the hedge fund's high fees and active management. This highlighted the premise that high-fee, complicated investments that try to "beat the market" by looking for misplaced opportunities can't compare with a diversified portfolio of simple, "plain vanilla" investments. It's worth noting that the true winner of this wager was Girls, Inc. of Omaha, who received the $1 million winnings. This is an organization in Omaha dedicated to empowering underprivileged girls so they grow up healthy, educated, and independent. How awesome is that?

HOW MAJOR DERAILERS AFFECT INVESTMENT MANAGEMENT

You spent time during the passions and pursuits piece figuring out what is important to you, which clarifies and prioritizes the goals that will be funded by the money you invest. Cash flow management tells you how much you

23   23 http://www.businessinsider.com/
warren-buffett-wins-million-dollar-bet-against-hedge-funds-2018-1

have to allocate into investments, once you have funded your fixed expenses, the discretionary expenses that are meaningful to you, and the long-term goals you've determined to fund. The cost of a particular goal will also tell you how much you need to generate from investments to fund it. In addition, the time horizon around that goal will dictate how you invest your money. For example, if you want to retire in five years, your investment strategy will look very different than someone retiring in twenty years.

Finally, business and career management then help you leverage your business or career to maximize the money you earn, so that you can put more aside toward your goals and maximize your quality of life. Understanding how your investment options relate to the rest of your accounts (non-retirement and retirement) will help you create a comprehensive investment strategy, one that is tailored to your unique goals and time horizons.

Be sure to maximize the options you have when it comes to your 401(k). Forty-seven percent of all women's primary source of retirement income is from employer accounts for savings and investments.

ANY STEPS YOU TAKE CAN MAKE A DIFFERENCE

You work hard for your money—you should be able to keep as much of it as you can. Having a strategy around minimizing taxes can make a big impact on your life. In addition, how you invest that money to pay for your goals can make a difference.

It's normal to feel overwhelmed—taxes and investment management are the most daunting parts in the whole financial planning process. (Keep in mind that there are careers dedicated to them.) This is why it's so important for you to bring in experts in these areas. Taxes are ever-changing, complex, and incredibly important to maximizing our income, and investing is an equally complicated and foreign subject for most. Having good resources in place to help you is the first step toward lowering your tax burden and getting your investments more in line with your goals.

TAX STRATEGIES AND INVESTMENT MANAGEMENT: STRATEGICALLY MANAGING TAXES AND INVESTMENTS TO ALIGN WITH YOUR GOALS AND MAXIMIZE FUNDS TO PUT TOWARD THEM.

- Know your goals before making investment choices.
- Create an investment strategy that is unique to your personal goals, risk tolerance, time horizon, and your investment philosophy.
- Maximize tax deferral options and minimize taxable income by taking advantage of tax-advantaged retirement accounts, health savings accounts, and other employer benefits.
- Reduce your taxes by choosing investments that are tax-efficient, lowering taxable income by maximizing deductions, utilizing the best personal tax filing status, applying business losses and expenses strategically.
- Locate your investments in the most tax-efficient account (asset location).

PART III

CHARTING YOUR COURSE

ROADMAP TO YOUR BEST LIFE

In this part, you will find guidance for creating a tailored, written plan of action for achieving your financial goals. This plan is dynamic in nature, and once implemented, it should be routinely evaluated and revised to ensure that it evolves to accommodate the changes in your life. Ultimately, this part will widen your perspective to once again emphasize your individual quality of life as essential to the entire financial planning process.

CHAPTER SEVEN

CREATE, IMPLEMENT, AND ITERATE YOUR ROADMAP

OVERCOMING DERAILER NUMBER FOUR—BUILDING A PLAN OF ACTION TAILORED TO YOUR GOALS

This chapter explains how you can take the information and insights you've gained through the exploration and analysis detailed in Part II and distill them into a concrete plan of action, i.e., a roadmap. Fundamental to creation of the plan is the need for you to prioritize goals and make choices about what you are willing to give up to attain those goals. The plan is also dynamic, requiring that you review and iterate it often to reflect changes in your life and priorities. In many cases, successful implementation and maintenance of the plan will turn on building a strong team of external resources, including any or all of the following: CERTIFIED FINANCIAL PLANNER™ professional, CPA, career or business coach, life coach, estate planning attorney, insurance broker, and business attorney. It doesn't hurt to have a therapist as part of your team, as well.

THE ROADMAP

As I've mentioned before, once I've walked a client through the four-part process of creating a financial plan, I send them home with a roadmap in the form of a one-page plan summary. As they make progress toward their goals, they update this one-page summary. Some items on the roadmap get done quickly, while others stay on there for a while.

CLIENT

1. Where you are now
   - Net worth: $738,738 (Assets of $826.7-Liabilities of $87k)
   - Current Net Lifestyle Cost (all expenses plus unidentified surplus, plus retirement contributions less taxes): ~$216,100
   - Fixed plus Discretionary expenses = $149,000   Surplus = $50,000
   - Estimated Net Retirement Lifestyle Cost: ~$110,600
   - On pace to pay off mortgage in full in 5 years
2. Goals you shared
   - Work part time until you find something you like
   - Work full time until 67, or full retirement age
   - Focus on funding retirement
3. Gaps in reaching your goals
   - Current lifestyle price tag is unsustainable given income potential
   - Portfolio income at retirement may not be enough depending on retirement age, or lifestyle costs
   - Portfolio assets too low to provide for Retirement Lifestyle Price Tag
   - Underlying investments for life insurance policy too conservative
   - Current investments not well allocated and not allocated based on goals
4. Solutions:
   - You can retire at 60 with a retirement lifestyle price tag of ~$75,000 (this includes portfolio income and social security) IF:
     i. You are able to contribute $25,000/year toward your retirement goal until retirement. This could be a combination of Employer and Employee contributions
     ii. Invest $90,000 of your current savings towards your retirement goal
     iii. Reallocate portfolio for long term growth
     iv. Reallocate Allianz investments for long term growth
     v. Restrict lifestyle spending

5. Action Item Checklist
   - To be attached to plan presentation follow up email

1. Where you are now
    I.   Net worth: $126,225 (Assets of $151,890-Liabilities of $25,665)
    II. Current Lifestyle Price Tag (all expenses plus unidentified surplus plus retirement contributions): ~$70,250 net (Fixed plus Discretionary expenses = $55,510
    III. Fixed expenses =$30,450. Discretionary expenses = $25,060. Surplus = $8115
2. Goals you shared
    I.   Buy a home in 3 years (2020) for $600k with 20% down
    II. Have children in 3-8 years
    III. Have the option to work part time down the road
    IV. Continue to work at your current company for the foreseeable future
    V.   Have 3-6 months Emergency Fund
3. Gaps in reaching your goals
    I.   Current earnings do not allow for increased or sufficient contributions to goals
    II. No clear strategy to fund any goals
    III. Current portfolio allocation not tax efficient, not well diversified, in higher cost mutual funds
4. Solutions:
    I.   Sarah's ability to manage her career for growth and her ability to maintain a modest lifestyle will allow her to fund the goals that are important to her. We believe she will be successful in reaching her goals provided the following steps are taken:
        i.   Work until Full Retirement Age earning at least as much as currently ($96,000)
        ii. Allocate annual surplus of $8100 equally between savings for Emergency Fund and Individual account for House fund ($340/month to each goal)
        iii. Save $10,000/year beginning 2020 for house down payment goal, after Emergency Fund has been funded, and save for 5 full years. Goal of 20% down payment on a house valued at minimum $450,000. This savings, plus the investments in the individual account will be used for House down payment in 2025
        iv. Invest 401k funds more aggressively, and reallocate entire portfolio for aggressive growth
        v.   Max out 401k contributions from 2026 until full retirement age. Continue with annual contribution of $6625 until then
        vi. Increase liability coverage for auto policy

As you'll see, the roadmap is broken up into four sections. The first section shows where you are now, the goals you shared, gaps in reaching your goals, and solutions. It's basic numbers—a snapshot in time of where you are financially. It offers you a realistic look at your net worth, which is your assets minus liabilities. It offers an accurate picture of your current lifestyle cost, as well as the costs associated with retirement and other specific goals, like education planning or a house down payment.

Next, you'll identify gaps between the goals you've specified and your current financial situation. Maybe you're running a cash flow deficit that needs to be made up, either with increased income or decreased expenses. As you make progress on your plan, your gaps will change and evolve.

Lastly, you'll explore solutions for overcoming the gaps between your current status and your goals. Through cash flow tracking and management, you'll have increasing funds available to funnel into your goals. Along the way, you'll clarify strategies to implement in your career or business that help maximize your earnings while enhancing the quality of your professional life. You'll also become more strategic handling taxes and investments, so that you keep more of the money you make and the money you put to work will work best for you.

You may see that it makes sense, for example, to dial back contributions to a 401(k) and instead make increased contributions to a higher priority account. You may decide to explore restructuring your business in a way that minimizes your tax burden, so that you can invest those savings. You'll see where you need extra resources or support to help you make the best decisions in certain areas.

Once you've created the action steps that lead you incrementally toward your goals, you begin putting them in practice. But that doesn't mean you don't look at your plan summary again. Rather, you'll take it out to review periodically throughout the year to assess your progress and make updates as needed.

Your plan summary may not be as detailed as one I make for a client. However, it will still allow you to know where you are behind in saving for any particular goal, determine how much money you need for it, and decide how much to put aside each month. If you are currently working with a financial planner, you'll have even more detail to add to your plan summary. However, your plan doesn't need to be highly detailed in order to be effective. The objective is to determine the big picture action steps necessary to accomplish the things that are important to you. Remember, the industry norm is to send clients home with a fifty- to sixty-page document that they promptly put into a drawer and forget about. By putting the basics of your financial strategy into one simple page, you make it simple to stay on track. If you forget everything else that was discussed, all you have to remember is the action steps on this one page. It is your roadmap to reaching your goals.

BUILDING YOUR OWN ROADMAP

Once you've done the analysis around each major derailer, the culmination of the planning process is putting it all down on paper. I cannot emphasize enough how important it is for you to put your plan in writing. As mentioned earlier, a 2015 study from Dominican University in California found that 42 percent of people are more likely to achieve their goals if they write them down. A psychologist determined a neurological effect that takes place when people put their intentions in written form. This correlation is the purpose of the one-page document I give clients. Writing down your financial plan creates commitment, fuels positive engagement, and helps you remember and retain your intentions around it.

WHAT AN IDEAL PLAN LOOKS LIKE

No matter how detailed a financial plan might be, the template I use for the plan summary is very parsed down. It is meant to force your thinking into four concise categories—where you are now, where you want to be, gaps, and solutions—because it simply won't be meaningful or actionable if it's unwieldy. It should simply be a matter of plugging in the numbers, then sitting back and clearly seeing the incremental solutions that are available to you. That's why the plan summary includes a checklist of action items. It shows clearly what you have to do, along with the actions that need to be taken by various members of your support team. It lets you know what needs to be done, when it needs to be done, and who's going to do it.

SET TIME HORIZONS

Choosing how you allocate money for goals is based on when you would like that goal to be reached. Likewise, you're going to have to prioritize when you do action items based on when you need the goal. For that reason, time horizons are essential to include in your financial plan. The due dates on your plan summary will depend on the action checklist, and that changes.

CHALLENGES WOMEN FACE WHEN CREATING A PLAN

The biggest challenges that women executives encounter when creating a plan is accepting the necessity of setting priorities, making choices, and making certain sacrifices in order to accomplish their goals. You're not alone in having this truth to deal with. As stated earlier, no one can have everything at once, no matter how much money they make. You have to think about what is most important for you, prioritize those goals, and make choices about what you're willing to give up to pursue them.

The second challenge is putting a plan together and implementing it—actually putting pen to paper and then doing it. I have plenty of clients who have plans and action steps, yet I have to continually push them to cross those items off their list. It's important to stay focused on what you want to accomplish.

The other great thing about the concise nature of this plan is that you can (and should) keep it someplace nearby. I advise that clients keep their plan in a place where they spend a lot of time looking, such as next to their computer. Keep the plan handy so you can easily access it, as well. As mentioned earlier, there also are certain apps you can use for monitoring cash flow. Whatever you choose to do, don't just stick the plan in a desk drawer and forget about it—it can't work for you if you don't engage with it on a regular basis.

Remember, this is an incremental process. You're not going to get everything done in just a few months. I recommend making it a point to sit down with your list of action steps at the beginning of every month and ask what one thing you can do this month. I know if you spend the time checking in with your plan and implementing your steps consistently, you will live the life you want on your terms. That's the entire purpose of the plan, even if you just make one change. Incremental change will add to the quality of your life.

NO TWO PLANS ARE ALIKE

Everybody's plan is completely different. You will have different goals, different steps you're working with now, and different challenges from anyone else you know. You'll also have a different team of resources in place to help you. As an executive, you are really good at whatever it is you do, but you're not an expert in these other fields, and you have to accept that. You might be a highly skilled attorney, but that does not mean that you're a CPA or a career coach.

I usually give referrals to help clients assemble their teams. You can reach out to friends and ask people you trust who they might refer you to. But don't just take a referral's word for it. Interview the people who are recommended to you until you find the best fit for your unique needs. In the Appendix, I've included a list of good questions to ask potential members of your financial support team.

CHOOSE YOUR TEAM CONFIDENTLY

When seeking out professionals to serve as your financial support team, don't be afraid to interview more than one person for each role. Women executives can sometimes feel obligated to work with someone simply because they spent a lot of time on your initial consultation, or because you had a good rapport. Remember, however, that in creating a financial support team, the most important thing is that *you* feel confident in the expertise and reliability of each person you work with.

YOU WILL HAVE TO MAKE CHOICES

If you find that despite your best efforts, you cannot afford to do everything you want, it isn't a reason for discouragement. Understand that having to make choices does not mean you're a failure—it means you're normal. Everybody has a limited amount of resources to work with, which means that everyone has to make choices. The fact that this is an incremental process means you always have plenty of time to think through your choices, try them before you fully commit to them, and make adjustments as you go. Every single step you take is an incredibly positive move toward living the life you want on your terms.

It's also important to understand that your roadmap is dynamic. As much as it provides clear guidance and action items, it also has to be flexible enough to respond to life changes. Jobs change, interests shift, life takes unexpected turns. You're going to have to check in with your plan to see how you've progressed on the action items and ask yourself if anything needs to be changed. The rule is every time there's a big change in your life, you have to go back to square one. You're getting married? Go back to square one and reformulate your passions and pursuits as a couple. Changing jobs? Go back to square one and ask how this affects your income, your benefits, your tax liability and your investments. Had a child? Got divorced? Sold your company? Go back to square one and reassess.

WHEN IT COMES TO YOUR PLAN, CHANGE IS A GOOD THING

To be honest, it would be cause for alarm if your plan didn't change over time. I've had people come to me with plans they had created years ago but that had never evolved to reflect their changed life. While it's great that they had a plan in place at that time, it may not have much to do with their lives today, ten years later.

I have an executive client who recently married for the second time and to someone where money was most definitely not important. As you might imagine, she makes significantly more money than he does. We had to talk about what that looks like from an estate planning perspective. If she should pass, how does her marriage change the way she'd like her assets to flow? Does it change the way she'd want to care for her son from a previous marriage? What are her goals now?

The other part of the conversation became about the joint goals she had with her new husband. This couple actually decided to sell their house in California as soon as her son goes to college and move to Minnesota, where her family is from. With so many exciting new goals in her life, we ended up doing a complete change of the action steps on her plan.

Financial planning is not a "set and forget" kind of thing.

Life constantly changes, requiring your plans and your actions to change with it. Each step in the journey of building your dream life involves making a new choice about your finances. Making those choices along the way is a lot easier than trying to backtrack after you're several steps down the road.

Even if you don't have any major transitions, at the very least, you need to sit down and take a look at your plan every six months. As you review, ask yourself where you are now, and how your action plan has served you thus far. The success of your plan depends upon how engaged you are with it.

TRUST IN YOUR PLAN

I previously mentioned Diane, my sixty-two-year-old client who runs a law firm and who came to me with very little saved for retirement. In the last two years, she has saved $300,000 for herself, though not without sacrifice. It's money she was spending before and now she's not. Frankly, I still encourage her to save more. Still, I'm thrilled with the progress she has made. She is engaged with her plan, which gives her this great sense of peace.

This newfound peace has not only made her a vocal proponent of financial planning, but also has reawakened some of her creative personal passions. Now that her business is working for her, funding the long-term goals that are important to her, she has time to garden and cycle competitively, two things she loves to do. (And, I would add, that she's very good at.) She feels the freedom to pursue the things that balance her life and give her joy, because the other pieces are working.

Diane is just one example of a person who's now in a place where she feels like she's living so much more life on her terms. It speaks to the power of having a plan—just the knowledge that you're making any headway toward living life on your terms provides a feeling that money cannot buy.

CREATE, IMPLEMENT, AND
ITERATE YOUR ROADMAP

- Prioritize your personal, professional, and financial goals. Know where you want to go.
- Know where you are right now.
- Identify the gaps between where you are now and your goals. Are you being derailed by one of the key derailers?
- Put together solutions. Identify the personal, professional, and financial changes you need to make to reach your goals.
- Prioritize what you want to do. Put together an action plan, and incrementally tick off the action items on your list.
- Write it down!
- Put your team together: certified public accountant, career/business resources, CERTIFIED FINANCIAL PLAN-NER™ professional.
- Revisit the plan at least every six months. Make changes as life and goals change.

CHAPTER EIGHT

SUPPORT YOUR JOURNEY

LIVING YOUR BEST LIFE

In my work with clients, I have found that what drives women executives' desire for financial security is not a desire for more money but for their best life. You cannot live your best life if your quality of life is not optimized. Thus, a large part of what I offer my clients, and the wider community of women executives, is continuing education and support around several key contributors to quality of life, including physical health, mental and emotional wellness, pursuit of causes important to them, and finding a community of like-minded peers. Exploring and embracing these elements will increase your quality of life in the here and now, and thereby support your journey to your best life.

NEED FOR COMMUNITY

When I write a blog post, I tend not to focus solely on financial matters. Believe it or not, I've found that my audience isn't likely to read many of those posts. But when I write something that deals with quality of life—whether that be six tips on living a healthier life, or easy ways to boost your nutrition—there's unbelievable interest. One of the most read and shared posts I've ever posted on LinkedIn was a piece on mindfulness.

It's been amazing to me how interested women executives are in this topic. It tells me that they are looking for ways to make their life better. The best way to do that is incrementally. Small changes can add so much to your quality of life.

As I've continued to host focus groups with women executives, I've learned a lot of great information on how to serve women executives better. I've also found that women executives crave these opportunities to come together as a community. They love the ability to talk with other women who understand and relate to their experience at this high professional level. If those opportunities include useful information that can help them live better lives, all the better.

Women executives have the career, they have the income, they have the possessions. What they don't have is time.

At least, they think they don't have it. The more I work and interact with these women, the clearer it becomes that they give away all the time they have—to their families, their friends, and of course, their jobs. They're not willing to give themselves the same respect they give their own profession.

When you ask women executives what their ideal life looks like, the answer is never about working more hours. It's about living life on their terms, right now, not constantly putting it off until some future time when they can ride out into the sunset. Women executives want to experience meaningful quality of life in the present.

Whether women executives realize it or not, another big contributor to quality of life is feeling connected, rather than alone. So many women executives feel like they are the only ones experiencing fear, anxiety, shame, and embarrassment around their financial situation. There is simply no reason for this to be the case.

FINDING THE TIME

The fact that women devour my posts on topics like mindfulness shows me they're taking the time to read about these things. The bigger question, though, is whether they are in fact doing the things my posts suggest. They want the information, but they struggle with taking action on it.

I know from personal experience how easily the best intentions can be derailed. I remember signing up for a Deepak Chopra/Oprah thirty-day meditation challenge. The platform was simple—a reminder would show up on my computer, and all I had to do was click on it and begin twenty minutes of meditation. I did it the first day—followed the prompt, spent the time, and felt great about it. The second day, however, there was a glitch in the link. I've never been back since.

I keep trying different ways to implement this discipline into my life. I downloaded the Headspace app on my phone. It sends me reminders to stop and meditate; however, I usually end up ignoring them.

Women don't follow through on their "better life" intentions for the same reason that they don't sit down to create financial plans: we are all really busy. We work all the time and then get home and just want a glass of wine. Despite how much we want to go to the gym, make a healthy meal, read the book that's been sitting on our nightstand for ages, when we finally find ourselves with a little time and space for ourselves, we can think of a million things we'd rather do. (Or "need" to do.)

Executives spend 62 percent of their waking life working[24]—that leaves very little time for all the other things

---

24   Bridget Grimes, "Six Tips to Help Women Execs Live a Healthier Life." WealthChoice.com, May 22, 2017. http://www.wealthchoice.com/six-tips-help-women-execs-live-healthier-life/

that create quality of life. One of the first things to go for many women executives is health. A *Harvard Business Review* study on women in the economy found that two-thirds of respondents describe themselves as overweight, despite also describing fitness as a priority.[25] That statistic begs the question you may have often asked yourself: how do you fit in the things that matter most to you?

The answer is the same way you fit the most important things into your budget: through planning. Your schedule works in much the same way as your budget. By identifying where you're overspending your time, and building incremental changes in how you spend your time, you can find time for all the things that enhance your quality of life.

The first step is finding hidden time slots. Studies show that there are consistent times when most busy professionals have availability, like Saturday and Sunday mornings, Fridays after work, Monday mornings, and Monday through Thursday evenings. By tracking where you spend your time, just like you would track your budget, you can identify the places where you don't spend time in a meaningful way and reallocate those slots for the activities you want.

Let's say exercise is important to you. Track your time for two weeks and see where you can find time to do it. Once

---

25   Michael J. Silverstein and Kate Sayre, "The Female Economy." Harvard Business Review. September 2009. https://hbr.org/2009/09/the-female-economy

you've found one or two possible time slots, schedule your exercise session in for four weeks, and see how it goes.

Don't try to do a full lifestyle makeover in those four weeks. You're much better off starting small with an activity you actually enjoy, and being consistent, especially while testing out how that activity fits into your schedule.

It also helps to find some way to hold yourself accountable. That could mean having a friend join you for that same time slot, or it could mean using a Fitbit or another activity tracking device that shows your progress in real time.

Finally, follow the 80-20 rule. Most women are familiar with this rule in regard to nutrition, but the principle extends to just about any activity you're trying to build into your life. If you stick to the plan 80 percent of the time, you can cut yourself some slack on the other 20 percent. I went to lunch with a friend who is trying to do the "Whole 30" diet. She confessed that after our lunch, she would be restarting the program for the fourth time in the last four days. "Every time I eat, I blow it and have to start over," she said. I had to tell her that this approach made no sense to me. What's the good of a lifestyle change if you never get past the first day? No matter what you're trying to build into your schedule, know that you're going to have transgressions, and that's okay. Quality of life doesn't have to be all or nothing.

QUALITY OF LIFE CONTRIBUTORS

Things that contribute most to our quality of life include physical health, mindfulness, pursuing a cause of deep importance, increased financial literacy, and relationships.

PHYSICAL HEALTH

Most women executives treat their careers and clients with more respect than they treat themselves. We always come last. Just look at the aforementioned Harvard Business Review study that shows how many women executives are overweight versus how many say fitness is a priority. Don't forget to schedule time for yourself and respect your personal life the way you respect your business and your career.

Prioritizing your physical health does not mean a complete 180-degree change overnight, nor does it mean forcing yourself to do things you hate. I have one client who used to get up at five every morning to visit the gym. While she might have been more physically fit, this habit left her feeling sleep-deprived and put her in a bad mood that lasted her entire day. Needless to say, it's important to find a fitness activity and a time slot that contributes to your quality of life, not detracts from it.

A great personal trainer who spoke to my women executives group advised that they start making time for fitness by carving out just ten minutes from their day and using it to take a ten-minute walk. That may seem like too small an increment to make a difference, but the benefits it yields will build up to big changes over time.

MINDFULNESS

Jon Kabat-Zinn, the father of mindfulness in this country, defined mindfulness as "paying attention in a particular way on purpose in the present moment and nonjudgmentally." He says one of the primary ways to cultivate the skill of mindfulness is through the formal practice of meditation. Neuroscience informs us that the consistent practice of mindfulness primarily through meditation results in measurable changes in the brain. It's about paying attention to where you are right now.[26]

There's an emphasis on being aware and happy with where you are in the present, not worrying about the past or the future, and living for right now. Western culture totally dismissed it until around 2010 when there was actual neurological proof that mindfulness is tied to making people not only happier, but more productive.

One of my trusted resources is a woman who is the direc-

26   Bridget Grimes, "Mindfulness: Christy Cassisa Speaks with us on the Awesome Benefits." WealthChoice.com, February 1, 2017. https://www.wealthchoice.com/mindfulness-christy-cassisa-speaks-us-awesome-benefits/

tor of the mindful integration program at the University of California, San Diego and founder of the Institute of Mindful Works. She spoke to my group earlier this year and showed that even a few minutes of regular mindfulness practice has wonderful benefits. It really does enhance our quality of life, and it's something that can be done incrementally.

PURSUING A CAUSE OF DEEP IMPORTANCE

Helping others gives you a greater sense of fulfillment, whether you give financially or of your time. Studies have shown that volunteering helps people who donate their time feel more socially connected. And according to a study from Carnegie Mellon University, volunteering time may provide physical health benefits like lower blood pressure and longer lifespan in addition to lowering stress. In fact, your overall well-being is found to be more enhanced when you do something for someone else.[27]

INCREASED FINANCIAL LITERACY

I'm a huge proponent of financial literacy and education—it's why I write. I hope the information I share gives women the confidence to take control of their financial

---

27   Susan Krauss Whitbourne, PhD, "Five Proven Keys to Improve Your Well-Being." Psychology Today, December 28, 2013. https://www.psychologytoday.com/us/blog/fulfillment-any-age/201312/five-proven-keys-improve-your-well-being.

lives. Continuing education has some terrific benefits for women. It is a key to increasing your well-being. Not only does it provide for social interaction and new skills, but it also provides an increase in confidence and goal setting, two huge factors that affect your success for living life on your terms.[28] Globally, it has been found that women are less confident than men when it comes to financial literacy, and this is true regardless of the level of education or socioeconomic levels. They are also less educated on the basics of finance. This combination of lack of confidence and lack of knowledge directly affects how women invest. They tend to be much less aggressive than men, which means avoiding growth investments like stock, leading to portfolios with lower returns.[29] Having less money for our goals directly affects our ability to live life on our terms.

RELATIONSHIPS

There's a lot of talk around the beneficial nature of relationships when it comes to choosing the right spouse or partner. But the benefits, and the importance in whom and how you choose, aren't limited to romantic relationships. Connecting with people around you is one of the five keys to well-being according to the NEF (study cited

28 Sam Thompson, Jody Aked, "Five Ways to Well Being: New applications, new ways of thinking." New Economics Foundation, July 5, 2011.

29 Tabea Bucher-Koenen, Rob Alessie, Annamaria Lusardi, Maarten van Rooij, "Women, Confidence and Financial Literacy." European Investment Bank Institute, February 2016.

previously). It has been linked to our mental health and happiness. Supportive, encouraging relationships that you find to be important to your own sense of meaning in life can provide you with fulfillment, well-being, and a greater sense of purpose in life. It points to the vital role that relationships play in human development at every level, from infancy to old age, and in every sphere of our lives.[30]

Women in particular crave personal relationships. It seems that we are uniquely oriented toward collaboration; we gain confidence and power from leaning on each other. We experience vulnerability not as a weakness but as a strength. Our informal relationships determine who we go to for advice or help with problem solving. And women are more likely to choose to collaborate with other women than with men.[31]

As a professional, you need a tribe of like-minded women whom you respect and relate to. I've personally borne witness to the things that happen when women executives come together to share challenges, obstacles, and best practices. Personally, I try to find a reason to get women together every month, even if all we do is have a glass of

---

30 Susan Krauss Whitbourne, PhD, "Five Proven Keys to Improve Your Well-Being." Psychology Today, December 28, 2013. https://www.psychologytoday.com/us/blog/fulfillment-any-age/201312/five-proven-keys-improve-your-well-being.

31 Brian Amble. "Collaboration and Gender." Management Issues, June 1, 2012.

wine and share our hard times or successes. That's what networking is all about—finding people whom you connect with and offering support where it's needed.

The benefits hold true even for women who work in the same industry and see each other as "competition." I meet with a peer group once per quarter that recently gained two new members, one of whom is a CERTIFIED FINAN-CIAL PLANNER™ professional just like me. After our first meeting, she reached out to me and asked whether I would prefer she transfer to a different group. I told her that as far as I was concerned, being in the same group was an advantage, not a threat. It offered a wonderful opportunity for us to support and learn from each other.

I haven't always felt this way. Earlier in my career, I did view other women as my competition. Looking back, it makes sense—having worked in male-dominated indus-tries, women were considered outsiders. But as more women slowly entered my industry, collaboration and support was more available. I see the same thing hap-pening in other industries—women professionals are becoming more open to sharing, less threatened by their peers, and more confident in who they are.

Personally, I love spending time with women who do what I do. It's been a great thing for me, especially in the years when I was launching my firm. In the process of due diligence, I reached out to people I knew and respected, who ran financial planning firms. They were very open about sharing challenges and resources, and I built my firm around a lot of the resources and feedback I got from those people. This spirit of collaboration is why I recently launched Equita Financial Network with my business partner and fellow CFP® professional, Katie Burke. The benefits women executives provide one another through collaboration are nearly limitless.

With the financial industry evolving so fast, I couldn't do what I do without having these conversations with my peers. It would be such a lost opportunity if I avoided them all out of fear of competition. I'm a firm believer that there are enough business and clients for everyone. I would rather we help each other and be seen as resources for each other. It's a tactic that has tremendously enhanced my business, and it is the motivation behind our new firm Equita.

MAKING TIME FOR QUALITY OF LIFE

While it may seem like you don't have the time to do any of this, taking the opportunities you have to make small changes to your quality of life are more than worth it. It may feel as though concentrating on things like health or community is taking time away from your career pursuits; however, improving quality of life supports rather than detracts from the pursuit of your personal, professional, and financial goals.

The fact is that when your business or career comes first, at all costs, your life is not gratifying. It's very sad and lonely. It's something we all know, or think we do. And it's incredibly unhealthy. The biggest killer of executives worldwide is heart attack, due primarily to a sedentary life and stress. Nevertheless, the statistics show that professionals in the highest levels have a hard time living in accordance with this truth.[32] One in four attorneys have alcohol abuse problems. Meanwhile, the internet abounds with articles, courses, apps, and other resources for finding balance in life. We need to be reminded that quality of life isn't a future benefit. It's something we are meant to experience now.

WAYS TO INCREMENTALLY ENHANCE QUALITY OF LIFE

Whenever I engage a speaker to talk to my community discussion group, I make it clear to them that their content needs to have two things: it has to make a difference in these women's lives, and it has to be incremental. I tell them that any advice they give these women will only be

---

32   Adrian Kennedy, "Corporate Wellness: A Cardiac Risk Profile of the CEOs," Apollolife.com, 2010. http://apollolife.com/CorporateWellness/CEOHealthandWellnessSurvey.aspx

successful if they can do it in manageable bites. They're too busy for anything more involved than that.

As a result, we've received some great practical training. Following are just a few of the techniques we've learned that can incrementally increase your quality of life.

NO TIME FOR THE GYM?

Let's start with the obvious: no one has time to go to the gym and work out. Nevertheless, the fact remains that heart disease kills one in three women. You can take short walks during the day. Get up when you take a phone call and walk while you talk. Split your desk work between standing and sitting. Help yourself stay accountable by using a fitness tracker or a friend.

NO TIME TO EAT HEALTHY?

A wellness expert at Kaiser Permanente who once spoke to my group about nutrition had some great tips for simple diet improvement. She said if you're too busy to cook complex, healthy meals, there are easy things you can do to better your nutrition, such as adding greens to a smoothie. It also helps a lot to prepare food the night before, so that it's ready the next day and you're less inclined to just grab fast food or eat whatever is around. Sign up for daily emails from health-based sources like GoRedForWomen.org.

New, easy recipes and reminders show up in your inbox daily and provide encouragement and resources.

You can take tiny little steps to incorporate healthy eating into your life.

NO TIME FOR MINDFULNESS?

A life coach whom I brought in to speak to my women's group shared with me that when he gets into his car to commute somewhere, he spends three minutes meditating, breathing deeply, and allowing himself to fully relax, before turning on the ignition. It's a small thing that sets the tone not only for his drive, but for his entire day.

There are a number of apps available for helping to cultivate mindfulness. Some send positive messages to you throughout the day and others guide you through meditation. I've included a list of my favorites in the Appendix—try a few and find one that fits your personality and lifestyle.

NO TIME FOR PERSONAL DEVELOPMENT?

I recently read an article that said scheduling just fifteen minutes of personal development time into your calendar can change your life. What counts as personal development? Anything that involves learning, cultivating your curiosities, putting yourself in a "student" position. The key here is to remember that personal development is a journey, not a destination. The point isn't mastery—it's the process that takes you there.

Any improvement you can make in your quality of life will support your personal, professional, and financial goals.

From the moment I began leading my small discussion groups with other women executives, I saw how much women wanted and needed this community. The group allows women executives a chance to share the authentic, sometimes unglamorous reality of life at this high-achieving level. It's tremendously inspiring to see like-minded women connect over their similar challenges and goals, bounce ideas off each other, and educate one another. Sometimes, all you need to get to the next level is to have others listen to you and relate.

Within this group, each woman can find a support network for the journey to her best life. Women in my group have confided about difficult moments in their marriages, parenting quandaries at every age, making the tough decisions at work and at home. When they do, other women in the group come to the rescue with empathy, practical suggestions, and creative solutions.

In many ways, this community functions a lot like therapy.

You can have a terrible day and let it out in a safe space, among people who understand exactly what you're going through. You can receive acknowledgment of your progress and praise for the ways you have persevered; this often provides the injection of hope you need to keep going.

SUPPORT IS CLOSER THAN YOU THINK

There are several places you can go to explore ways to start improving your quality of life. Whether it's an in-person community or an online community, there are endless places for finding the support network that you need to live your best life. You'll find a detailed list of resources in the Appendix.

In addition, every major city and region has more industry-specific women's groups than you can possibly imagine. Get on Google or Facebook, search under your location and field, and then start visiting a few. You don't have to belong to every single one, but find one that you like. Start there and see what grows from it.

FINDING BALANCE

A 2009 article by an expert in palliative care details the five messages she heard repeatedly from dying people.[33]

---

33 Bronnie Ware, "Regrets of the Dying." BronnieWare.com, accessed May 11, 2018. https://bronnieware.com/blog/regrets-of-the-dying/

None of them ever wished they had worked more. Instead, they wished they had chosen to spend more time with people who were important to them.

It's important to make sure you have a plan around a career that gives you the quality of life you want, not just the compensation. There has to be balance. Finding the quality of life you want requires introspection. You have to figure out what you want and how you can add little steps incrementally to enhance that quality of life.

SUPPORT YOUR JOURNEY: LIVING YOUR BEST LIFE

- Connect with a group of like-minded women for support, collaboration, and education.
- Allow for incremental change to enhance your quality of life, from wellness to financial security.
- Incorporate manageable, bite-sized steps of key quality of life benefits like meditation, fitness, volunteerism, and financial change.
- Keep learning. Choose delivery sources that work for you on topics that are important to your personal, professional, and financial goals.

CONCLUSION

This entire book is meant to inspire you with hope. By taking smart, simple steps to overcome the biggest financial derailers, and incorporating those steps into a plan, you will create power and purpose that moves you in the direction of your goals. In the plan lies the balm to the anxiety, fear, and shame that often accompany inaction and inattention to your financial situation. But with the method I've laid out in these pages, you now have a roadmap for your journey of action toward financial success, security, and your best life.

Let's go back to Sophie, the client I mentioned at the very beginning of this book. I talked about where she started, as well as the great place where she ended up. What I didn't mention, however, was that there were several years when we didn't get a whole lot accomplished for her plan. She was really unhappy with her life, but she didn't have a lot of confidence that small changes could help her get where she wanted to be. She tried to get satisfaction without focusing on making changes to her lifestyle or career—building a fancy home, working remotely, going on vacations. It was incredibly frustrating for her. None of it brought her happiness. She was getting nowhere because she wasn't ready to address the real issues.

After years of making no progress on curing her misery, she was finally ready to engage. She came to me and said, "I'm ready to do this. Talk me through what this is going to look like."

This was music to my ears. We got out her plan and went over it, line by line, making adjustments for how her goals had changed since the last time we reviewed it. We created a timeline together around those goals that would guide her in prioritizing her funds.

Then, Sophie got started. She scaled back her spending to ensure that she wasn't wasting any more funds on things that weren't meaningful to her. She began incrementally saving for the first big item on her list of goals: the house in Europe. She leveraged the job where she was making a lot of money, so that she was able to make even more, while saving significantly in her tax liability. Month by month, year by year, I saw her mood improve as she felt more in control of her daily choices while progressing on the path toward her dream life.

Now, when I talk to her, she tells me everything is going great. She still works a lot, but now she feels great about it because it's on her own terms—she's making the choices about her clients, her schedule, her workload. She's making more money than we ever anticipated, which makes it possible for her to save for retirement and invest at the same time. The more she saves, the sooner she will have the freedom to stop working as soon as she wants to.

I could not be happier about Sophie's story. It's so often that women executives like her have an opportunity to change their life but choose not to engage with the process and take the steps to get there. I really wanted to see her step up and take full advantage of the amazing opportunity in front of her. Now, she's so happy, and it's great to see her enjoying life. After all her years of hard work and planning, she deserves it.

KEYS TO BECOMING FINANCIALLY SUCCESSFUL

Living the life you want takes incremental change and smart, simple steps. You have to know about the four derailers, what they are, and how they can impede your ability to live life on your terms. You need to have a plan around how to avoid them.

Start with creating a picture of what you really want your life to be. Prioritize that picture—spend time thinking through the details of what is really important to you personally, professionally, and financially. Next, take a realistic assessment of where you are today, and write down the actions that will lead you, step by step, toward the life you want. Then, start managing your cash flow. Make meaningful choices with how you spend your money instead of throwing it into places that provide little satisfaction. Allocate your money toward goals that are important to you. Identify the opportunities for leveraging your career and make a plan for overcoming the challenges it presents. Assemble a team around you that can help you get where you want to go and surround yourself with a community of women who can keep you motivated along the way. Plan with incremental steps you can take to help you reach the goals and live the life that you want. Finally, write it all down.

I don't advocate that you save every dime and don't live for now. There has to be a balance between effort toward the life you want and enjoying the life you have. You have to manage your career or business, so it affords you not only the compensation that you want, but the quality of life you want, and those two things are not mutually exclusive.

THINGS TO CONSIDER AS YOU EMBARK ON THIS JOURNEY

There are some tips that will help you as you begin to make changes.

PLAN COMPREHENSIVELY

When you're creating your action steps between where you are and where you want to be, it's imperative that you really dig into the details. Your analysis will not be the same as the one I would do, but that's okay. You just have to know where you are personally, professionally, and financially, and understand how those areas are interrelated within your ideal life. As an executive woman, you are in a unique and enviable position of having a career you can leverage to accomplish your goals. You can leverage it for the cash flow you need to fund some of your goals. You have the income and the tools to do it. You just need to sharpen your tools and get them working for you the best way you can.

DIVE DEEP

The planning process starts with drilling down into your hopes, visions, goals, interests, and motivations, to really understand what's important to you. You must own the fact that in order to make progress, you will have to make choices, not only about which things are important, but about which things need to happen first, while choosing to wait on other things for a little while.

ENGAGE WITH THE PROCESS

No matter how detailed and comprehensive your plan is, it can never bring you success unless you engage in the process. Living life on your terms means being invested fully in each step you take toward your goals. You must revisit your plan every month, assess your progress, make changes if necessary, and seek out accountability to keep you committed.

EMBRACE INCREMENTAL CHANGE

Things don't happen just because you wrote them down on a piece of paper. You must be willing to make necessary changes. I always remind my clients after we've finished designing their plan that if they take it home but don't implement it, they've just wasted their time and money. Putting the plan into practice means changing some of the things you're used to doing. It helps to write the plan down and break it out in manageable pieces. That way, you won't be overwhelmed.

ENLIST HELP

You're not an expert in everything related to your finances. Fortunately, you don't have to be. What you do need to have is a team of experts in the right fields to work together on your behalf. A solid team of financial professionals will not only give you clear, manageable action steps, but will give you peace of mind that all your financial bases are being covered.

ATTEND TO YOUR QUALITY OF LIFE

Quality of life is about more than money—it's about choosing what's really meaningful to you and living on your own terms. The life you want, no matter what that might look like, is entirely within your grasp. Once you know what it is you want, you have the incredible freedom and power to make the choices that get you there.

If you want a meaningful life on your terms and financial freedom, you have to take care of yourself. Quality of life includes health and wellness, having relationships, and pursuing causes that are important to you. It's about you—you are important, and you are driving all of this.

HOPE FOR THE FUTURE

If there's one thing I hope that you take away from this book, it's the knowledge that you can do this. Financial planning does not have to be overwhelming. An ideal life lived on your terms is absolutely within your reach. You just need to focus on a couple key things.

There is power in the plan. Without a roadmap, you're not going to get anywhere. Once you have that roadmap and are committed to implementing it, you're on your way.

A lot of women feel shame, fear, and anxiety around money. By taking the steps laid out in this book, you can alleviate those feelings and move forward with confidence. Think of the stories shared in this book of people who implemented their plans and now feel better and can breathe easier. There's no shame in needing help. At every level in our economy, the people with the greatest financial security are the ones who have clear financial goals and are supported well in progressing toward them.

I hear it all the time from clients that just getting started on this process makes a huge difference in their quality of life. This is true even for those who come to me deep in debt, stressed out of their minds, and feeling like they have no time for anything else on their plate. After a week or two of working on their plan, even before they've saved a single dollar, they show up for our meetings with a remarkable change in their voice.

Over time, I've learned what that sound is. It's the sound of hope.

Hope is what I want you to feel now that you've read this book. You may have some of the derailers, but if you take just those first steps, you'll be on your way to living the life you want.

ACKNOWLEDGMENTS

Several years ago, I set out to write the book you now hold. The vision was there, the passion was there, but as often happens with life, things got in the way, and the book idea was set aside. However, it never really went away, and the desire stuck with me until the fall of 2017 when this book was started.

What I find so thrilling about the book is that like my own life over time and much like financial planning, the book I originally was going to write has evolved. And it would not be what it is now without the support and encouragement of some very special people.

I would like to thank my husband, Scott, for his endless support and faith in me for all the crazy ideas I have. For being my rock, keeping me focused, and grounded. For always encouraging me to back up and look at issues rationally. For completing me and truly bringing out the best in me.

To my parents, Rita and Michael Venus. Thank you for your constant encouragement, your suggestions, your belief in my vision to make a difference to women everywhere.

To my children, Miller and Marnie. Who knew my kids could be among my greatest supporters? Endless words of encouragement, praise, and honest feedback. I could not be more proud of your engagement in my passion to write a valuable tool for women.

To my sister and fellow entrepreneur, Sandra, who has been my sounding board for this and every project I have launched.

To my publishing team, without whom I could not have written this book. My scribe, Chelsea Batten, my outliner, Karla Bynum, and my editor, Julie Arends. Great women who organized my thoughts and turned my ideas into words, and my words into a book I am so very proud of.

To my clients. For sharing your lives with me, trusting me to guide you along your path and to help you live the best life you can, I thank you.

And to hard-working women everywhere. From you, I have learned that as women, we can pursue what we love, become financially secure, and live a full, meaningful life. For that, I am eternally grateful.

APPENDIX

We take our vision to help women take control of their wealth seriously. For this reason, when we come across excellent resources, we want to share them. We encourage you to comb through the articles, books, websites, and other material we have assembled for you. And if you have an excellent resource to share, please let us know, and we'll add it to the list!

CHAPTER 3

WEALTHCHOICE®

The key to better living

Passion and Pursuits Worksheet

1. **Where am I now?**

   Personally: family, spouse, children, passions, organizations, trusted advisors

   Professionally: my current position, organizations, passions

   Financially: salary, assets (retirement assets, home, bank accounts), liabilities (mortgage, debt), net worth, monthly cash flow

Please prioritize the top 3 most important passions and pursuits for you:

1

2

3

2. **Where I would like to be in 1, 3, and 10 years, prioritized**

	1 yr	3 yrs	10 yrs
Personally:			
Professionally:			
Financially:			

3. **What does your ideal life look like? Now and in the future?**

4. **What challenges do you think you need to overcome in order to achieve those passions and pursuits?**

5. **What help do you think you need/resources to successfully reach your goals and have your ideal life?**

Other considerations:

What is your definition of success?

Are there causes that are important to you?

CHAPTER 4

PERSONAL BALANCE SHEET   DATE

Assets

Cash Accounts
Savings $ -
Checking $ -
                                                    $ -

Taxable Accounts
Brokerage Account $ -
Trust Account $ -
                                                    $ -

Retirement Assets
401k Account $ -
IRA $ -
                                                    $ -

Life Insurance (cash value)
Insurance Policy $ -
                                                    $ -

Residential Real Estate
Home value $ -
                                                    $ -

Total Assets: $ -

Liabilities

Mortgage
Mortgage terms (x%, due when) $ -
                                                    $ -

Additional Loans (Car, Student)
Loan terms (x%, due when) $ -
                                                    $ -

Total Liabilities: $ -

NET WORTH $ -

PERSONAL CASH FLOW	Month	Month	Month
Net Income	$	$	$
Fixed Expenses			
Rent/Mortgage	$	$	$
Medical			
Groceries			
Homeowner Insurance			
Miscellaneous			
Utilities			
Phone/Internet/cable			
Gas			
Student Loans			
Garbage/Water			
Car Payment			
Childcare			
Home Maintenance			
TOTAL:			
Discretionary Budget			
Travel	$	$	$
Auto Service			
Cash/ATM			
Clothing			
Credit Cards			
Education			
Entertainment			
Health & Fitness			
Savings			
Dining Out			
Sports& Hobbies			
Kids			
Shopping			
Home			
Unclassified			
TOTAL:	$	$	$
Total Expenses:			
Surplus/Deficit			

SMARTPHONE APPS FOR TRACKING SPENDING

- YNAB
- Pocket Guard
- Personal Capital
- Good budget
- Everydollar.com
- Spending tracker

I also recommend J.Money's Excel budgeting template, "Budgets are Sexy." http://www.budgetsaresexy.com/free-budget-templates-sites/

DETAILED DOCUMENT CHECKLISTS FOR COLLECTING ALL DATA RELEVANT TO YOUR FINANCIAL SITUATION

- Investment and savings accounts
  - Bank account statements
  - Investment account statements
  - Employment benefits statement
  - Retirement/401k PSP plan statements
  - Stock Option/RSU/corporate stock statements
  - Charitable account statements
- Income information
  - Most recent tax return
  - Most current pay stub
  - Social Security benefit statements
  - Cash flow worksheet (see previous page)
- Liabilities
  - Mortgage value and terms
  - Home Equity Loan value and terms
  - Student loan value and terms
  - Car loan value and terms
- Insurance policies
  - Life insurance policies
  - Disability insurance policies

- Long-term care policies
- Annuity policies
- Auto policies
- Homeowner's policy
- Family information
  - Children's 529 accounts, UTMA/UGMA
  - Date of birth for family members

ONLINE CALCULATORS FOR COLLEGE EDUCATION COSTS

- College Board: https://bigfuture.collegeboard.org/pay-for-college/college-costs/college-costs-calculator
- American Funds: https://www.americanfunds.com/individual/planning/tools/ext/college-savings-calculator#
- College Data, College Match: https://www.collegedata.com/cs/search/college/college_search_tmpl.jhtml
- FAFSA4Caster: https://fafsa.ed.gov/FAFSA/app/f4cForm?execution=e1s1

LONG-TERM CARE COST CALCULATORS

- Genworth Cost of Care Calculator: https://www.genworth.com/sales-center/education/cost-of-care.html
- CNN: http://cgi.money.cnn.com/tools/elder_care/elder_care_cost_finder.html

- AARP: https://www.aarp.org/caregiving/financial-legal/info-2017/long-term-care-calculator.html

CHAPTER 6

QUESTIONS TO ASK WHEN INTERVIEWING A CPA

- How long have you been working as a CPA and what is your area of expertise?
- How do you add value to your clients?
- What other services can you provide outside of tax preparation?
- If I have a question, will you bill me for every email, phone call, etc.?
- Whom will I be working with—you or a member of your team?
- What is your fee structure?

QUESTIONS TO ASK WHEN INTERVIEWING A FINANCIAL PLANNER

- Are you a fiduciary?
- How do you get paid?
- Do you help people like me?
- What are your credentials?
- Will you personally advise me, or one of your staff?
- How often will we meet? Is there a charge for those meetings?
- How long do you plan to be in the business?

HIRING AN INSURANCE ADVISOR

- Ask people you respect for a recommendation.
- Interview prospective agents. Talk to them about your situation and see which ones take the time to listen and can explain the pros and cons in a way you can understand. The majority of agents work on commission. A knowledgeable and capable agent is paid exactly the same as an agent with little or no expertise.
- Look for an agent that has experience in the product you wish to buy. For example, your home and auto broker may sell life or long-term care insurance but has little or no experience in that marketplace. Look into the expertise of the agent; ask if they are able to show you several companies to help you with this type of coverage. Insurance should not be a "one-size-fits-all" experience.

HIRING AN ESTATE PLANNING ATTORNEY

Because estates can vary wildly in complexity, it's good to find an estate attorney who works with people like you. Because this is such a personal and often emotional relationship, you need to find someone you can speak to openly about your personal life and wishes.

Questions to Ask When Interviewing an Estate Planning Attorney

- Whom do you serve? What type of client base do you have?
- Will you collaborate with my financial planner?
- How much do you charge? (This also varies greatly.)
- Are you a specialist in estate planning or a general practitioner?
- How long have you been practicing?
- Do you also provide trust administration?

HIRING A BUSINESS COACH

There are two types of coaches. There are lifestyle coaches who motivate, inspire, and hold you accountable but do not focus on helping you with a specific situation. These are coaches you want to engage with when you know what you need, but you need someone to hold you accountable to get you off your butt until your behavior changes.

Then there are business coaches. These are specialists or systems coaches to engage with when you need a change specifically around your business.

Before setting out to find a coach, determine which type you need—lifestyle or business coach—and if you are a good candidate for coaching. You must be committed to the results you want. To get started, ask other businesswomen who are successful and whom you admire who their coaches are. As you interview different coaches, ask yourself whether the coach seems interested and caring about your situation. Go with your gut—it's critical to work with someone whom you feel you can trust.

Questions to Ask When Interviewing a Business Coach

- What diagnostic tools do you use and what is your process?
- Do you have experience in my area of business?
- Can I speak with some of your clients? Have you helped them successfully reach their goals?
- Will you give me some time upfront before I commit to working with you? (This offers a chance for you and the coach to try each other out before you engage.)
- Do you document my objectives and create a process to reach them?
- Do you require a long-term commitment? (Avoid this if you can.)

CHAPTER 8
APPS FOR CULTIVATING MINDFULNESS

- Headspace
- Insight Timer
- The Mindfulness App
- Buddhify

- Stop Breathe & Think
- Calm
- Smiling Mind
- 10% Happier

RESOURCES FOR FINDING A SUPPORTIVE COMMUNITY

Ted Talks on the importance of community

- Sheryl Sandberg: Why we have too few women leaders
- Casey Brown: Know your worth, and then ask for it
- Kirsten Hall: Women in business-entirely unremarkable
- Susan Colantuono: The career advice you probably didn't get

Women's Groups

While this list is by no means comprehensive, it offers you a start of where to look locally.

- AAUW-American Association of University Women
- ABWA-American Business Women's Association
- AFWA-Accounting and Financial Women's Alliance
- AMWA-American Medical Women's Association
- AWIS- Association for Women in Science
- CREW-Commercial Real Estate Women
- Ellevate Network

- EWI-Executive Women International
- HBA-Healthcare Business Women's Association
- LWV-League of Women Voters
- Lean In
- NAFE-National Association for Female Executives
- NAWBO-National Association of Women Business Owners
- SWE-Society of Women Engineers
- Soroptimist International
- WITI-Women in Technology International
- Women Corporate Directors
- Women President's Organization
- Alumni organizations
- Industry-specific women's organizations
- Religious organizations
- Philanthropic groups
- Political groups
- Sports-related groups

OTHER RESOURCES

BOOKS

- *Women's Worth* by Eleanor Blayney
- *The Intelligent Investor* by Benjamin Graham
- *Lean In: Women, Work, and the Will to Lead* by Sheryl Sandberg
- *Women Don't Ask: Negotiation and the Gender Divide* by Linda Babcock and Sara Laschever

- *The Male Factor* by Shaunti Feldhahn

ARTICLES

- DailyWorth.com articles by Bridget Grimes
  - "The One Gift to Give Yourself for a Better 2016," December 2015
  - "How to Make Your 401(k) Work Best for You," November 2015
  - "How Liking Your Job Can Save You Money," August 2015
  - "The Financial Perk of Being Single," June 2015
- "The Confidence Gap" by Katty Kay and Claire Shipman, *The Atlantic*, http://www.theatlantic.com/magazine/archive/2014/05/the-confidence-gap/359815/.
- "Why Women Still Can't have it All" by Anne-Marie Slaughter, *The Atlantic*, http://www.theatlantic.com/magazine/archive/2012/07/why-women-still-cant-have-it-all/309020/.
- "Women and the Labyrinth of Leadership" by Alice Eagly and Linda L Carli, *Harvard Business Review*, https://hbr.org/2007/09/women-and-the-labyrinth-of-leadership.

FAVORITE FINANCIAL BLOGS AND WEBSITES FOR FINANCIAL INFO

- WealthChoice.com
- Catalyst.org
- Wiserwomen.org
- DailyWorth.com
- Nerd's Eye View, http://kitces.com
- GenYPlanning.com
- WorkableWealth.com
- J.Money, http://budgetsaresexy.com
- Wife.org
- HBR.org
- WorkLifeLaw.org
- McKinsey.com
- DRI.org (specifically their Sharing Success online newsletter)

A FEW OF WEALTHCHOICE'S TRUSTED RESOURCES

- Roger Lane, www.rogerlane.com
- Karin Blair, https://www.evokinginsights.com/
- Marianne Trost, www.thewomenlawyerscoach.com
- Marcy Morrison, http://careerswithwings.com/
- Pamela DeNeuve, http://pameladeneuve.com/
- Gaylene Xanthopoulos, http://theleadershipedge.com/

- Christy Cassisa, mindfulness coach at Institute for Mindful Works
- Simon Sinek

ABOUT THE AUTHOR

 **BRIDGET VENUS GRIMES** is the founder and president of WealthChoice, a firm focused on helping women turn their professional success into financial success. She is also a cofounder of Equita Financial Network, Inc., a network of independent, women-led financial planning firms that share best practices and common goals. As an advisor to top-earning female executives, business owners, and attorneys, Bridget draws on more than a decade of experience to create customized financial solutions that help her clients achieve the life they long for. Based in San Diego, California, Bridget enjoys cooking, entertaining, and spending time on the water in the company of her husband and children.